Lacy Sunshi

Precious Fairy Boo's (

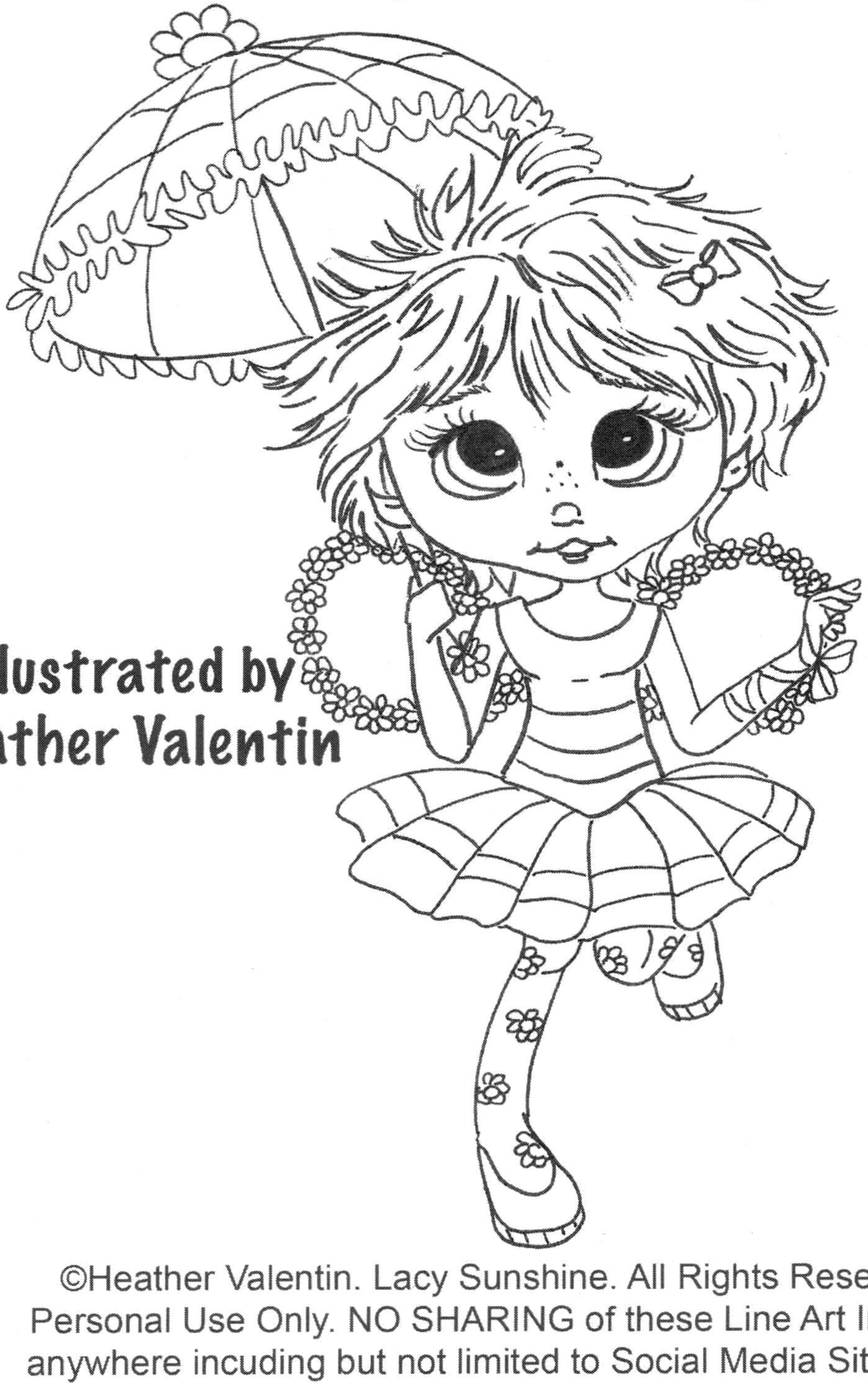

Illustrated by
Heather Valentin

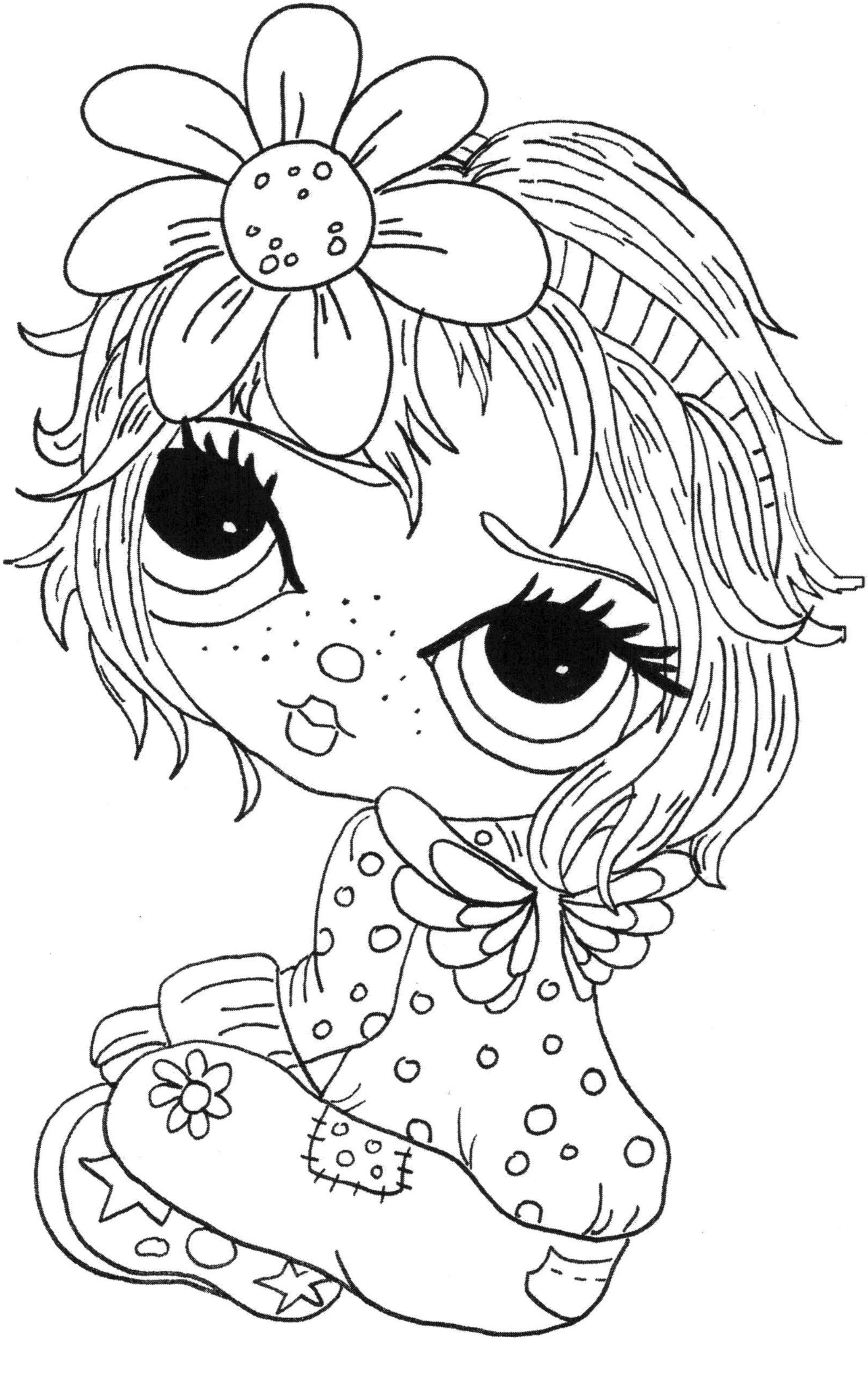

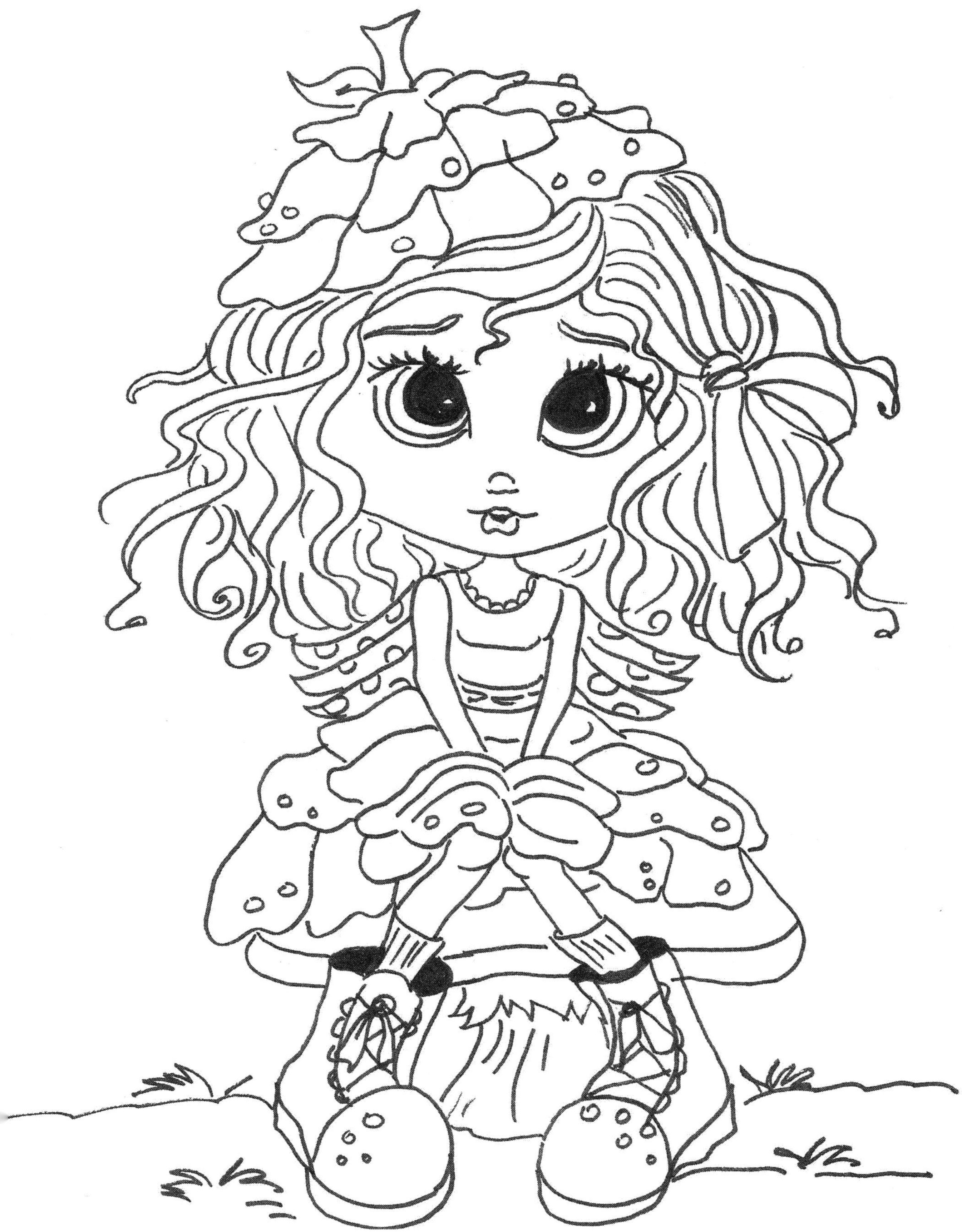

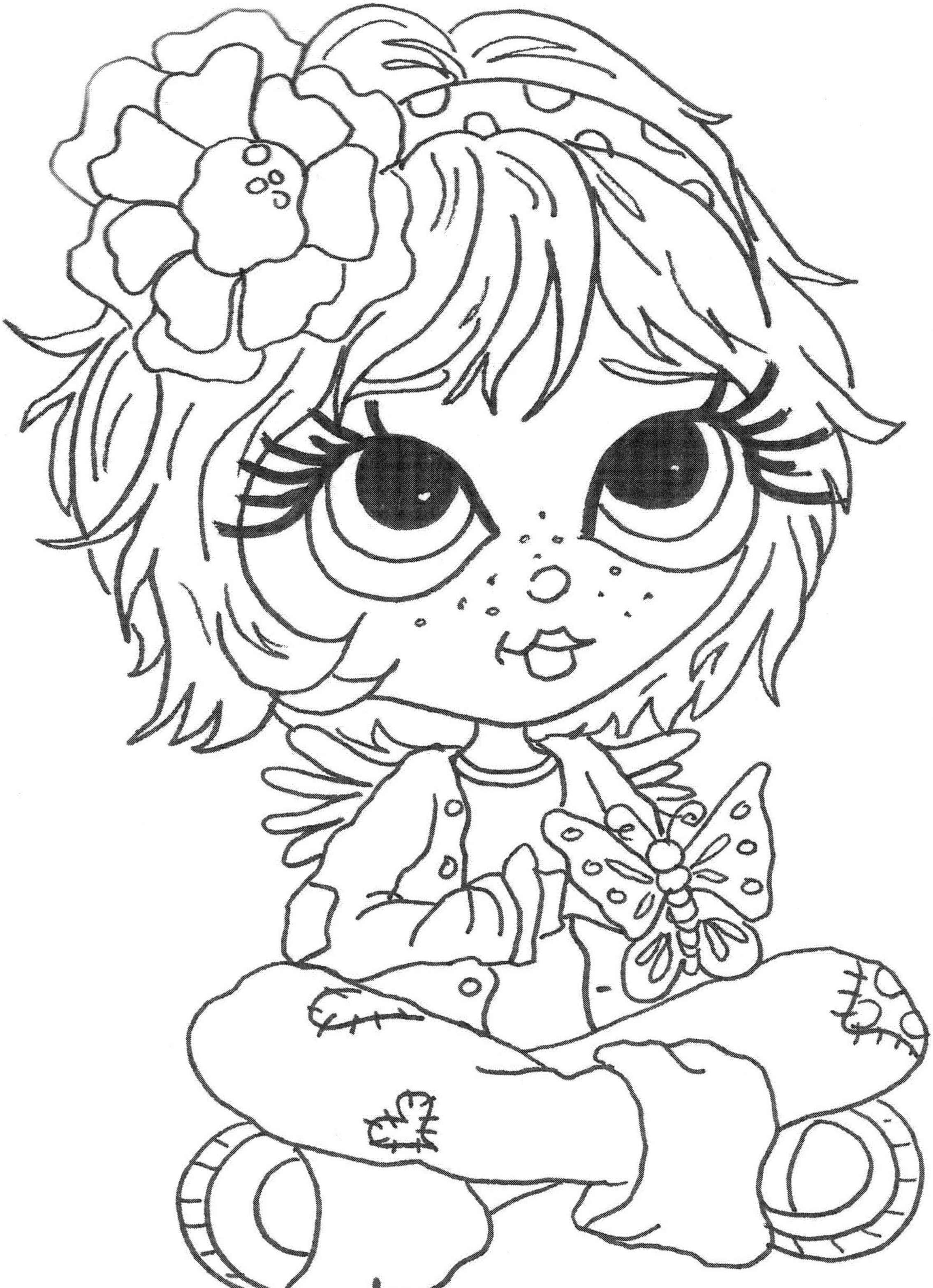

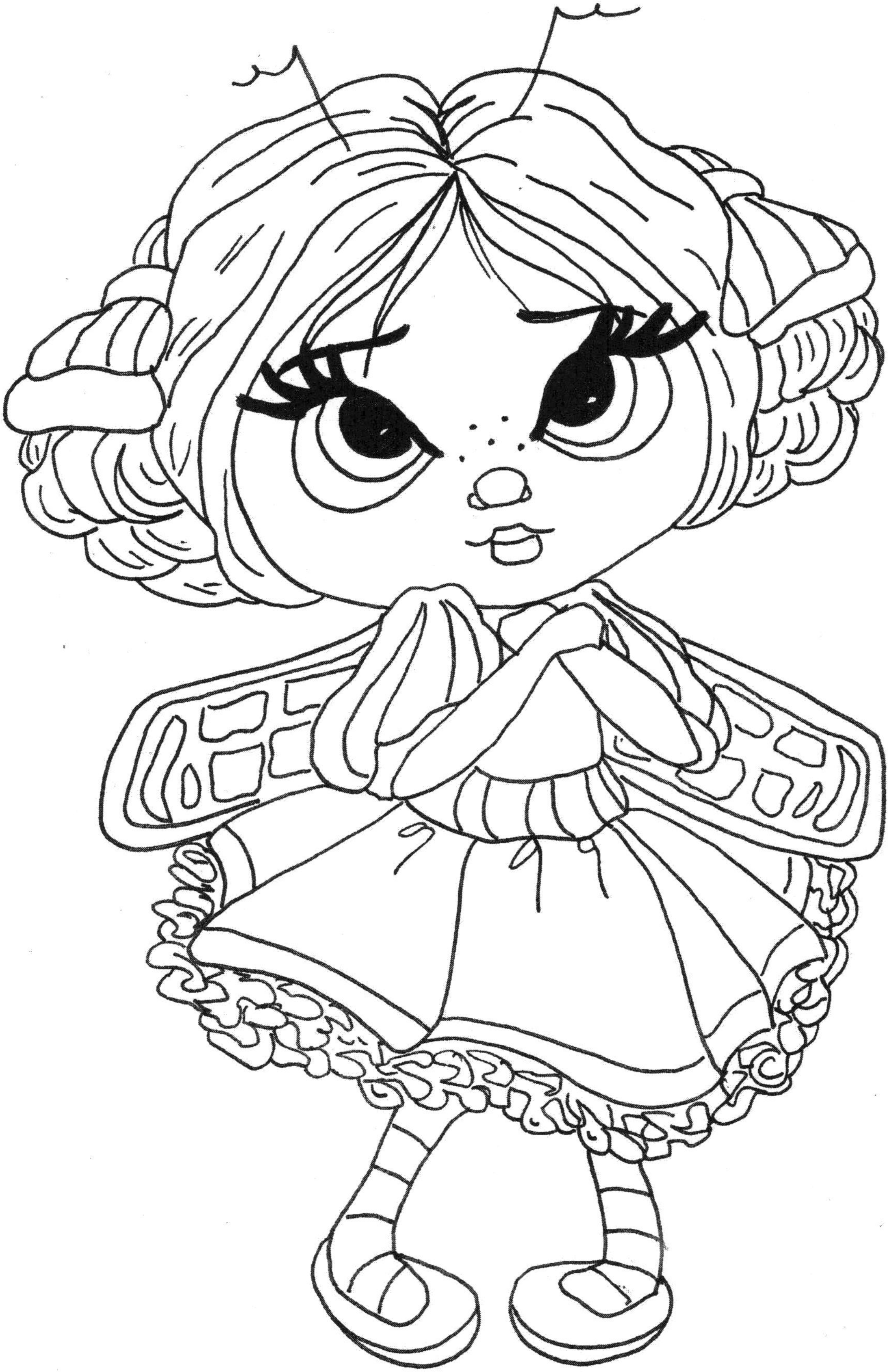

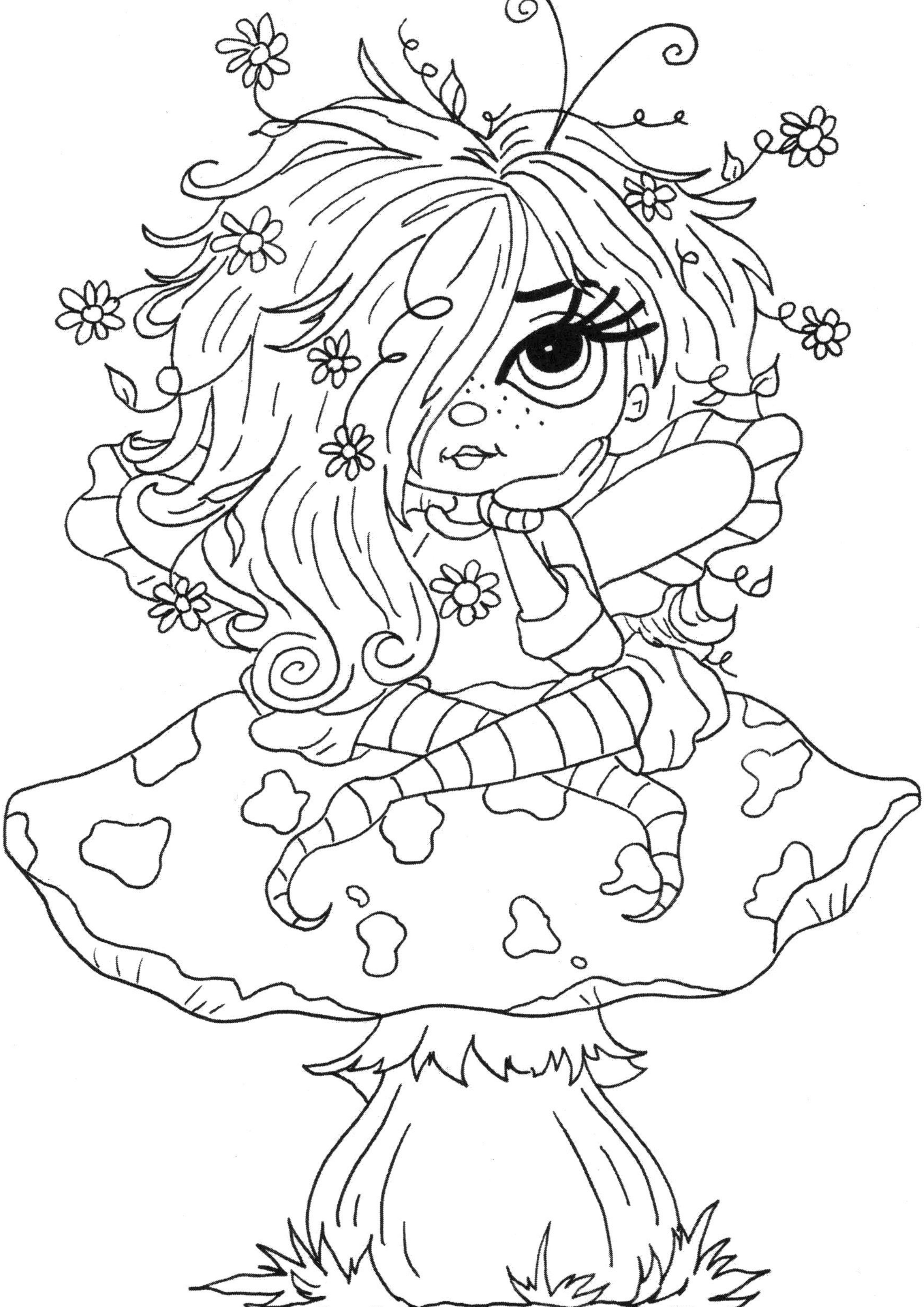

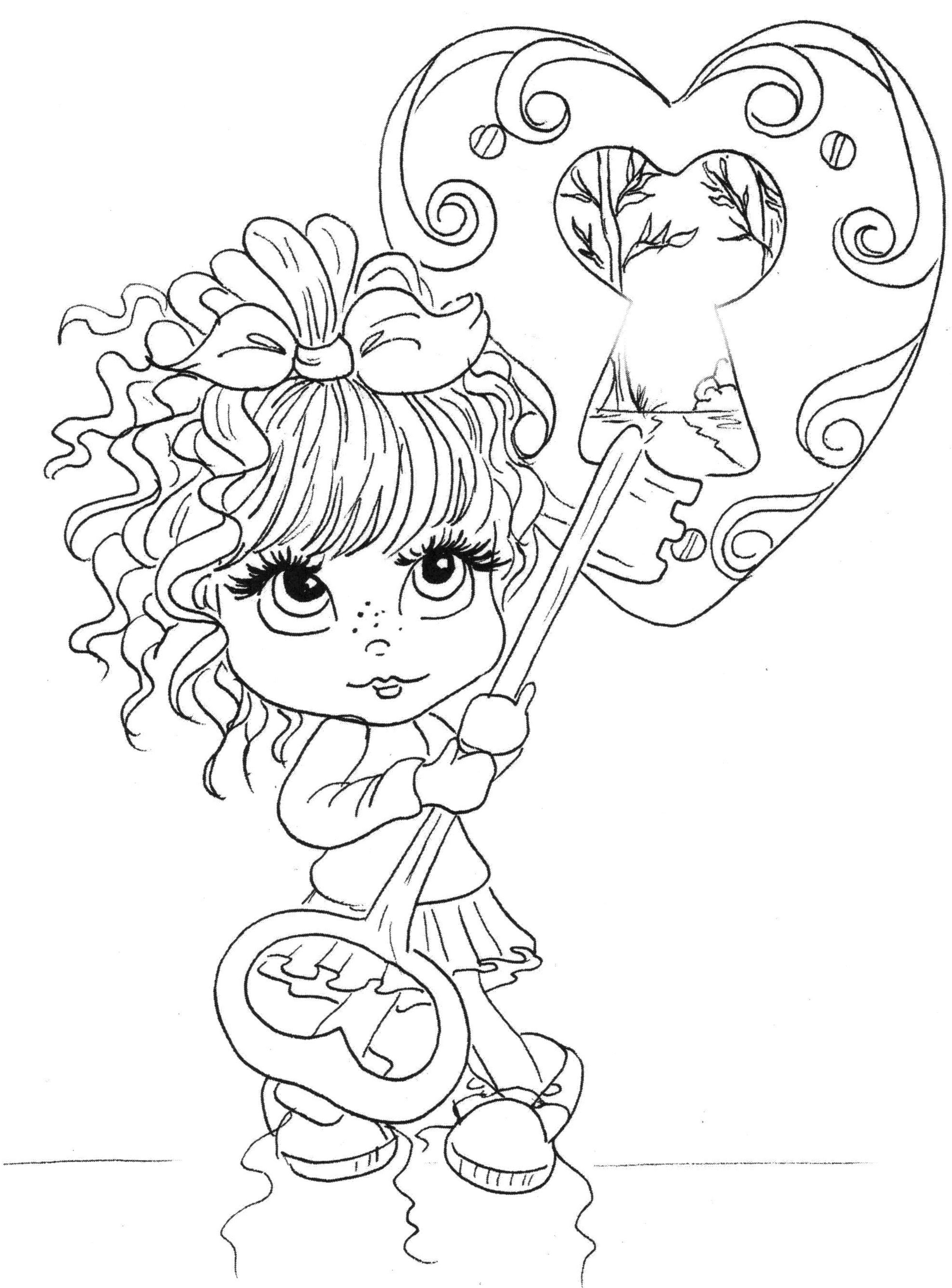

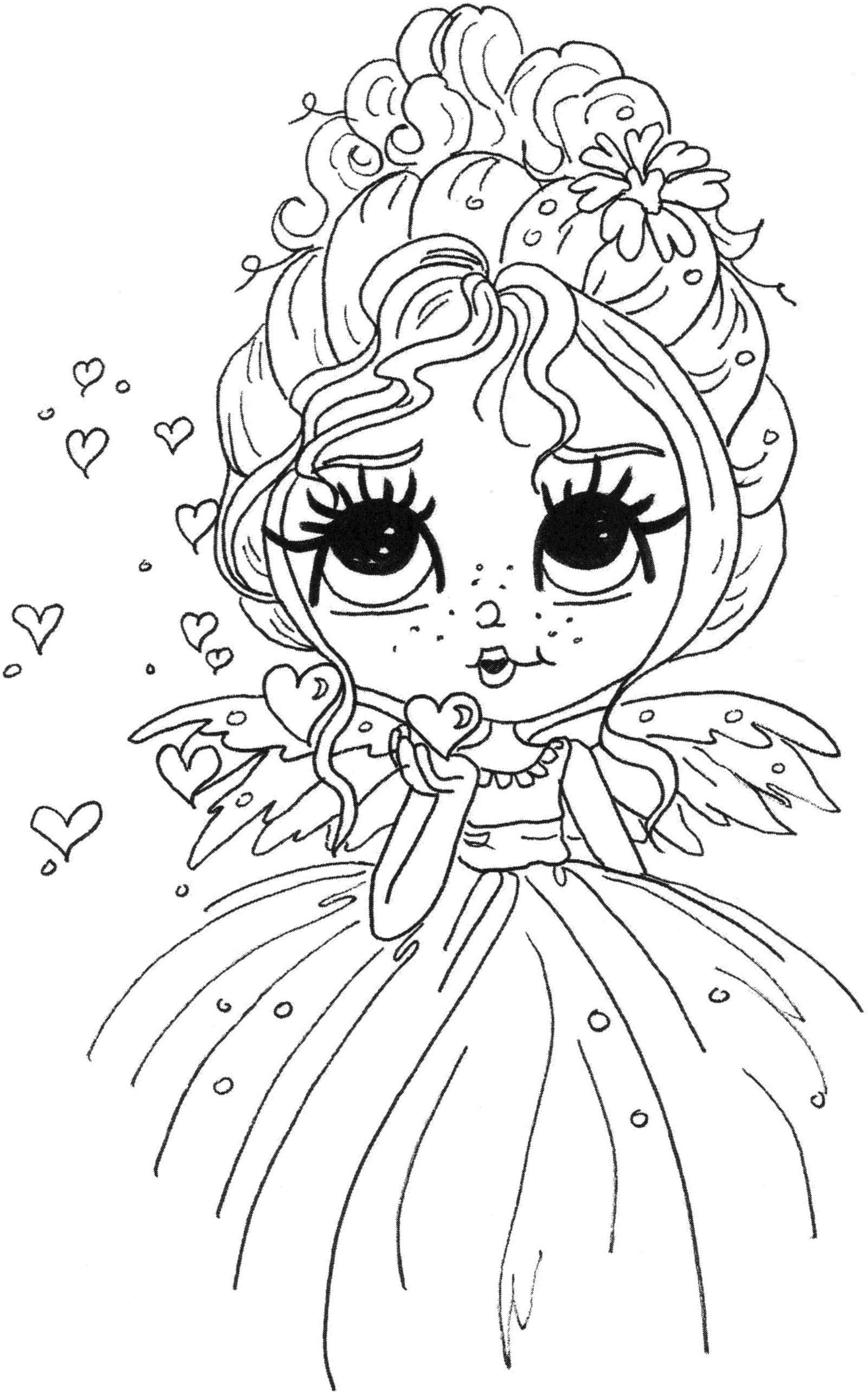

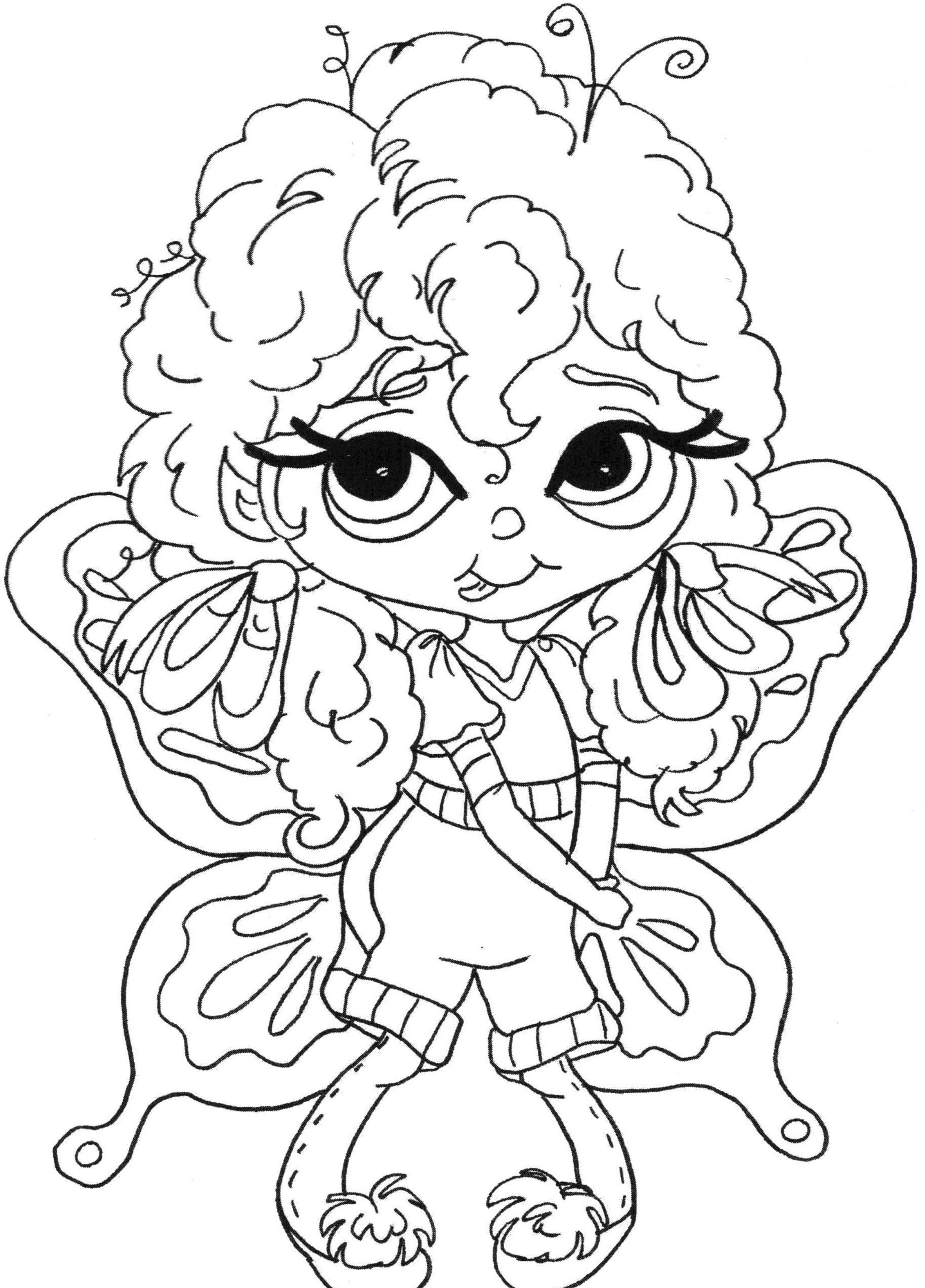

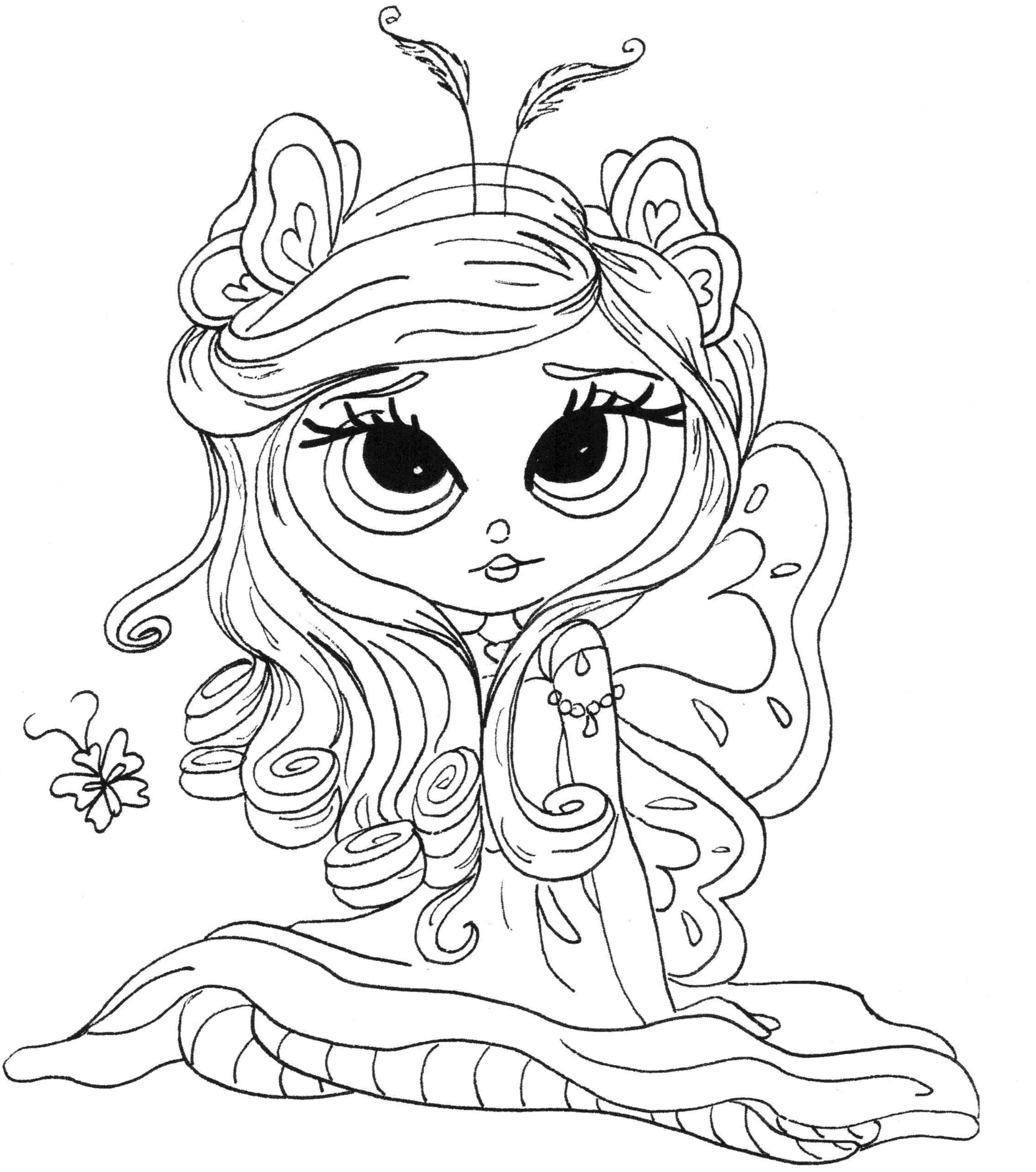

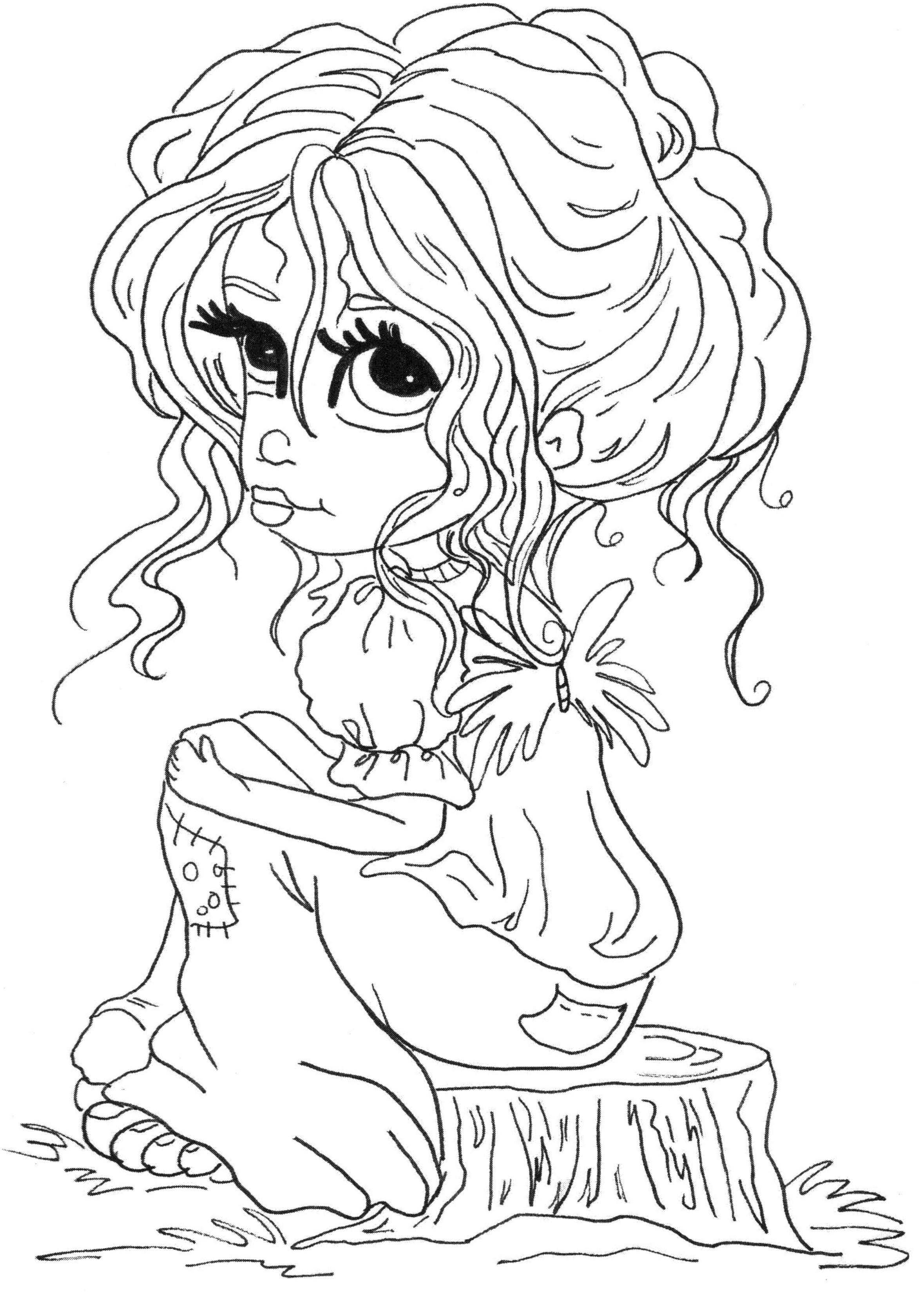

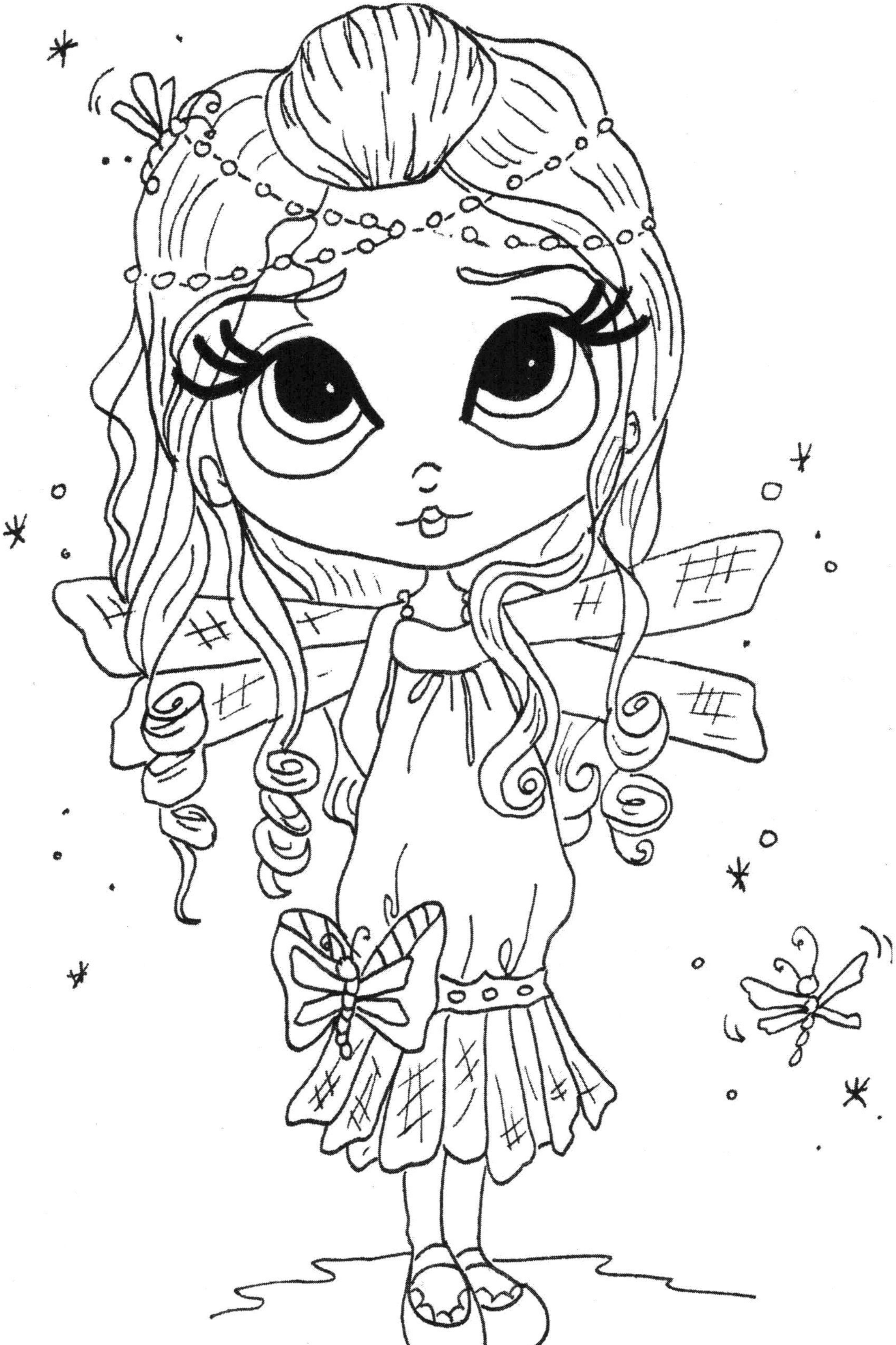

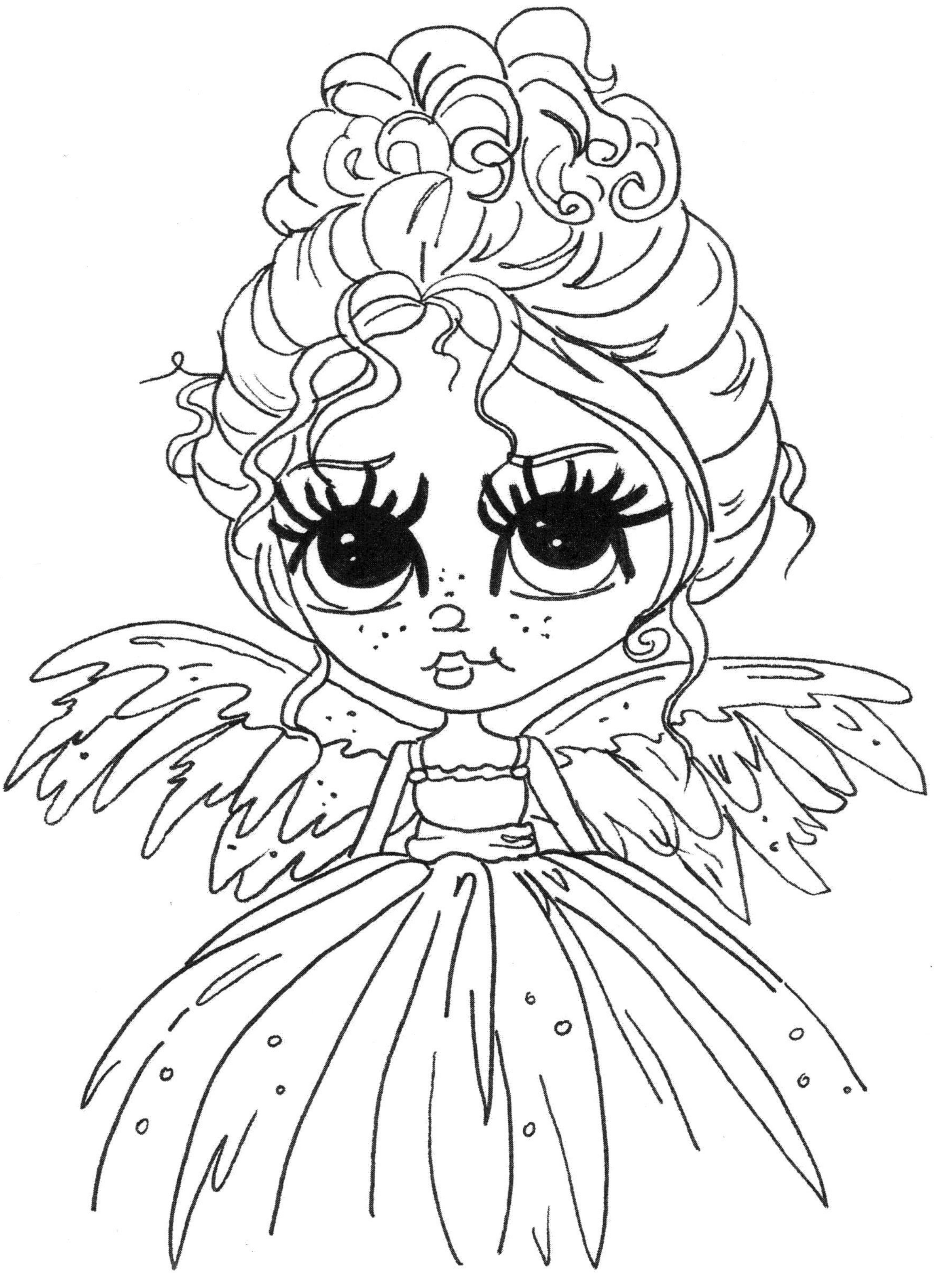

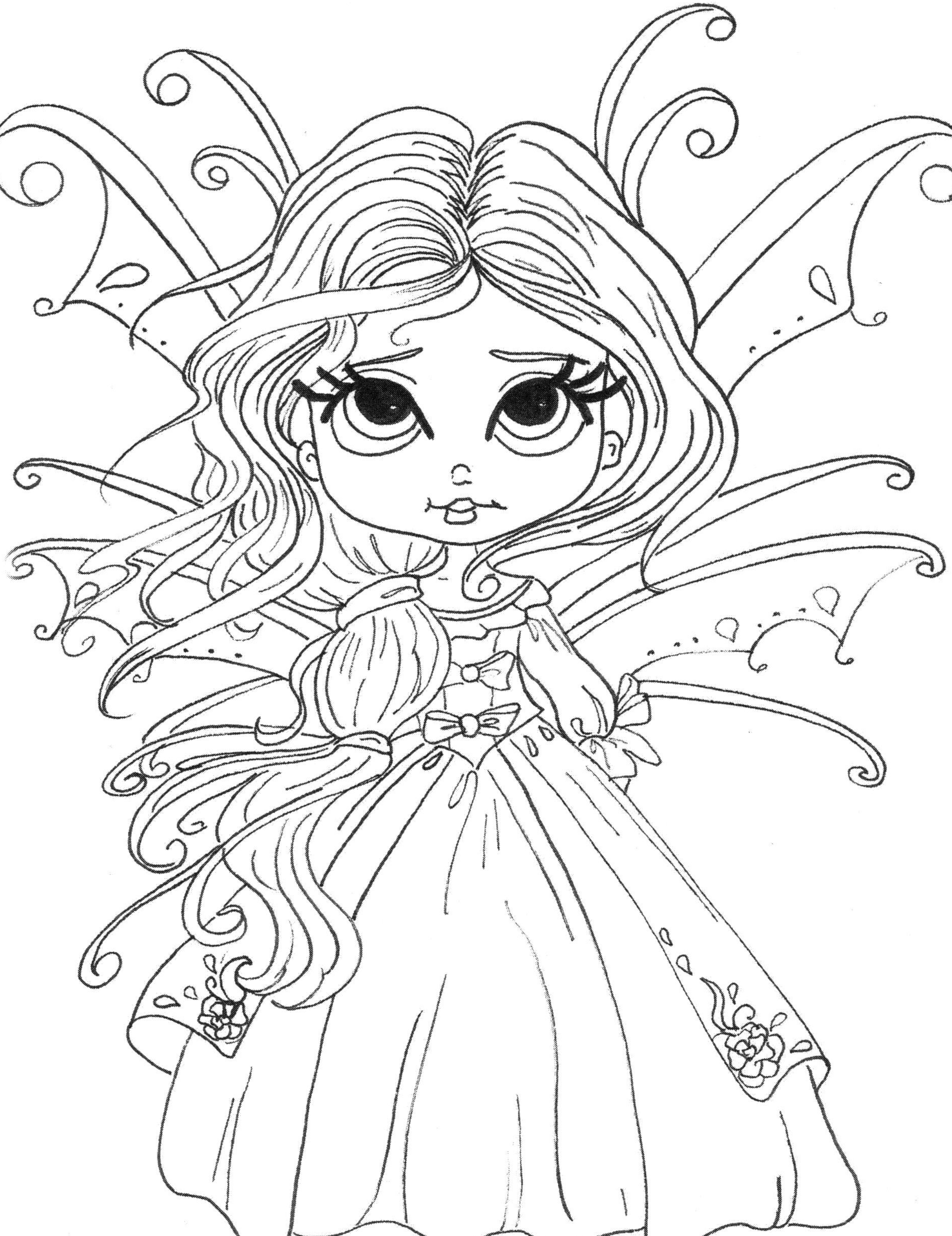

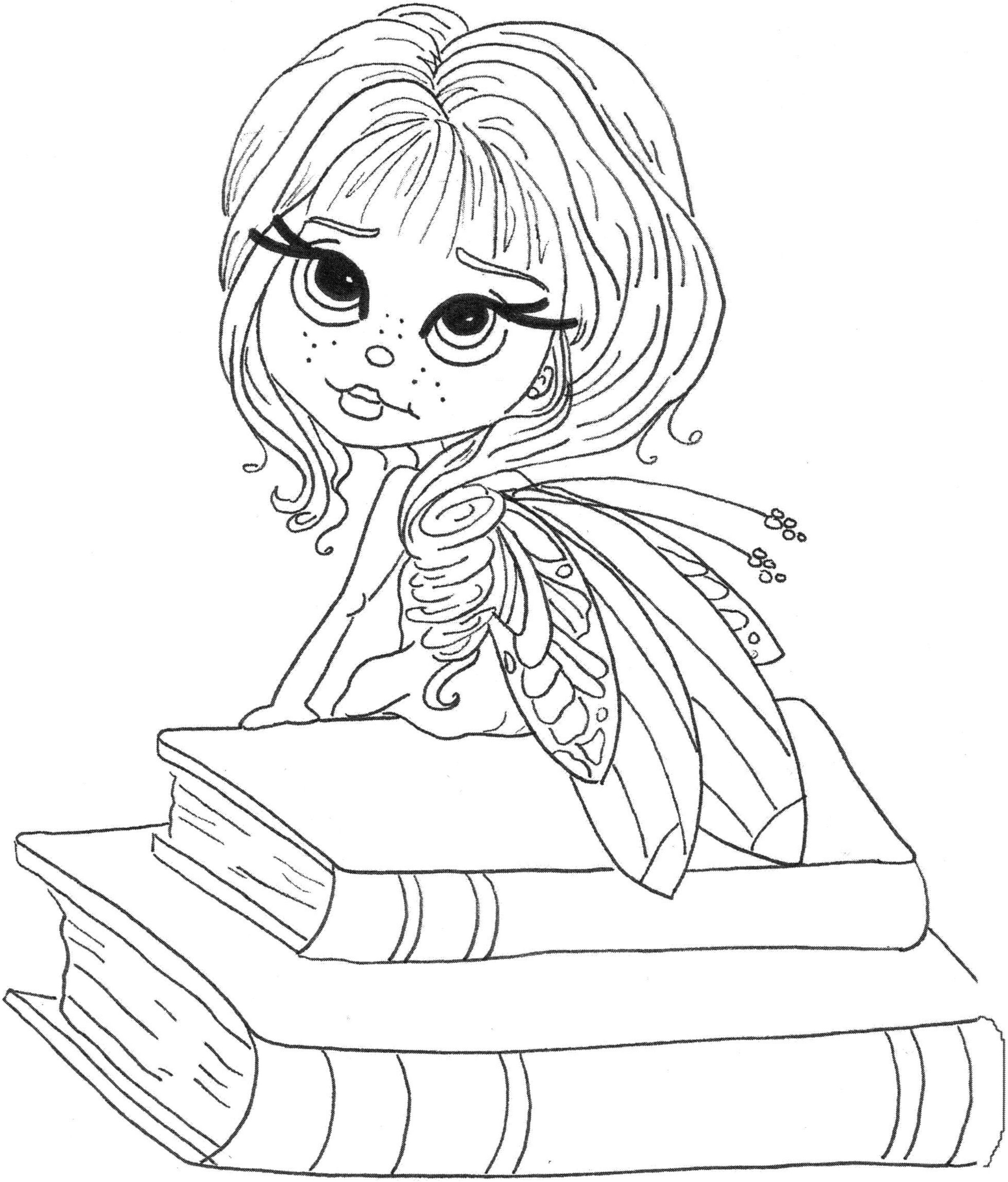

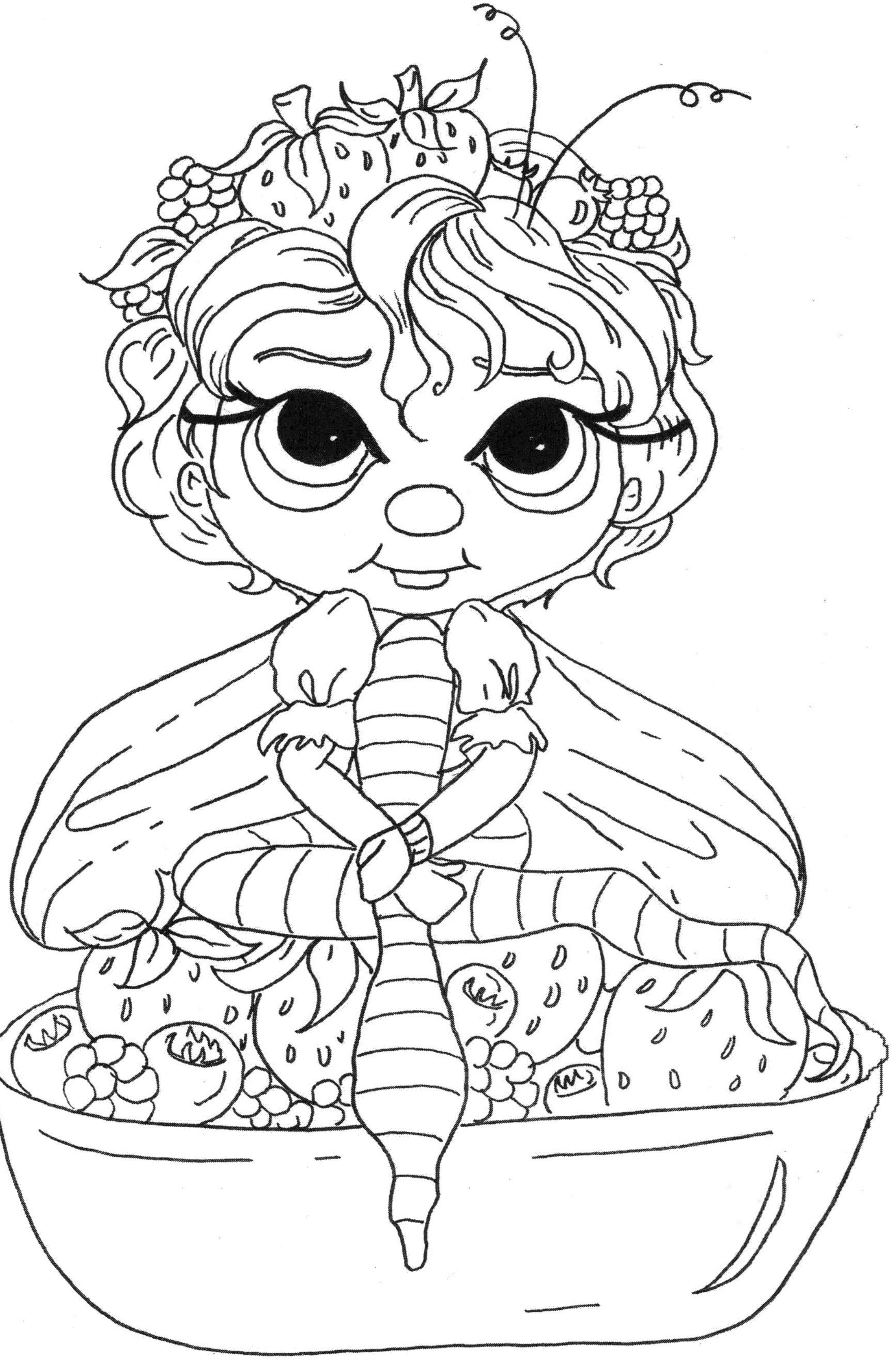

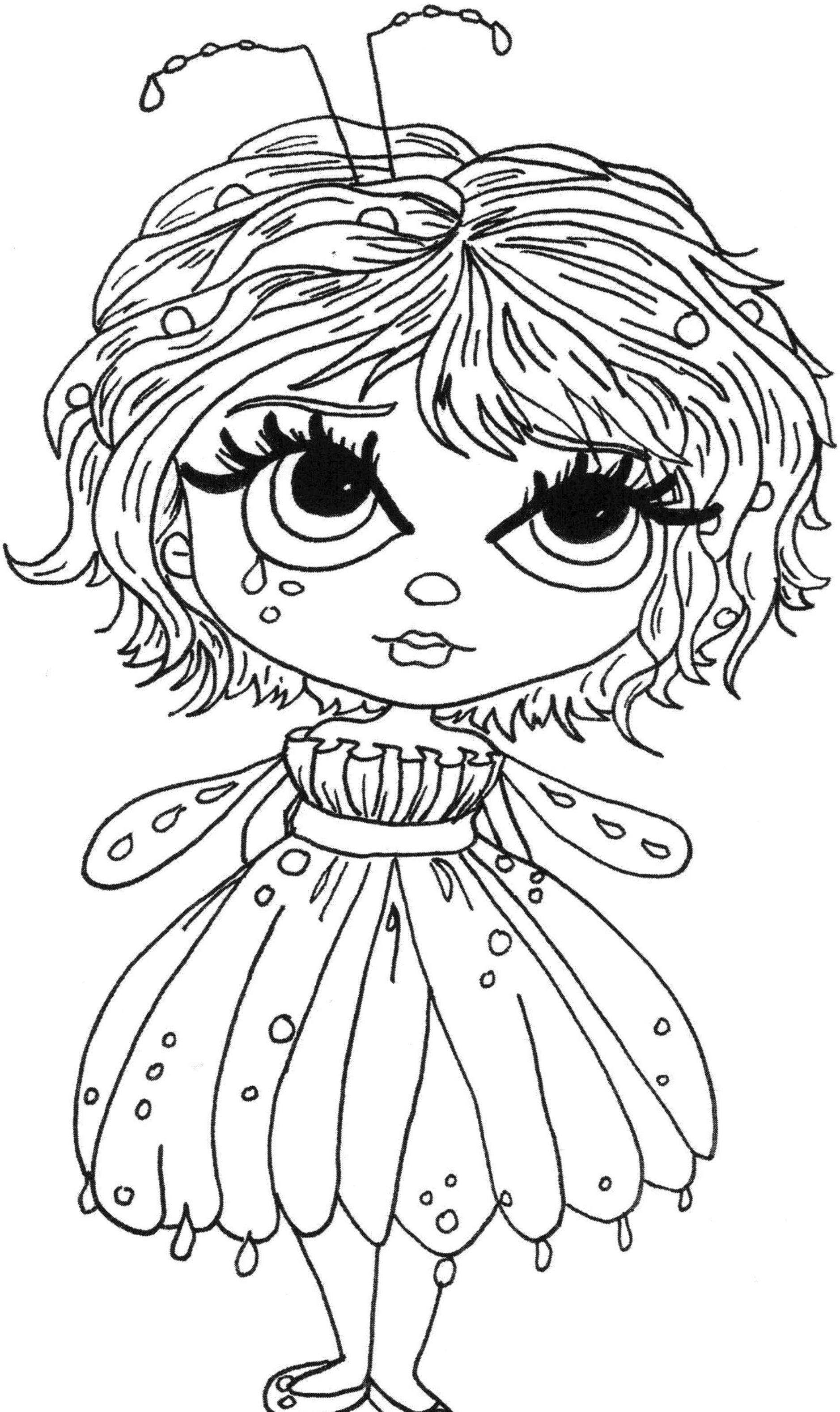

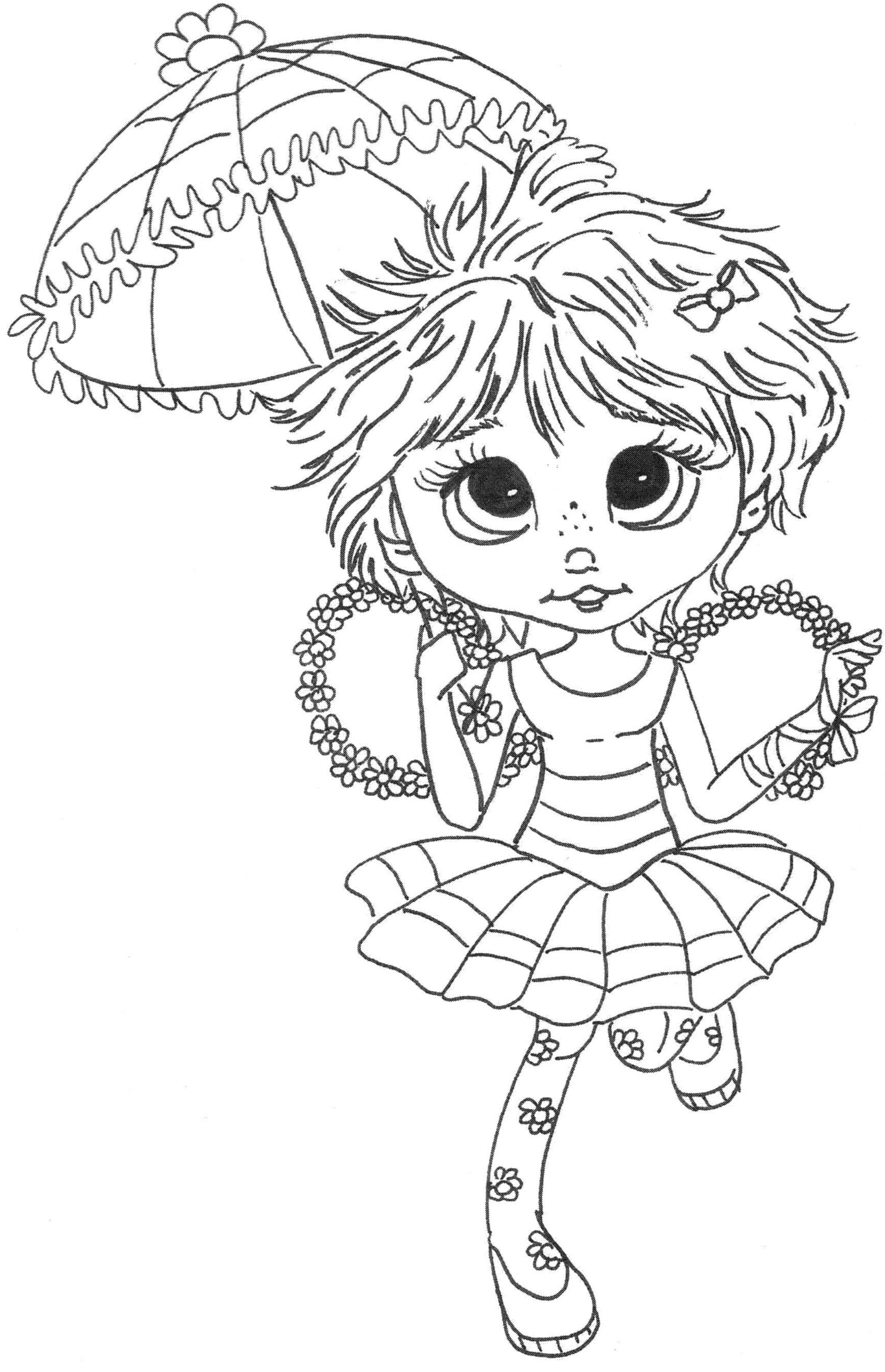

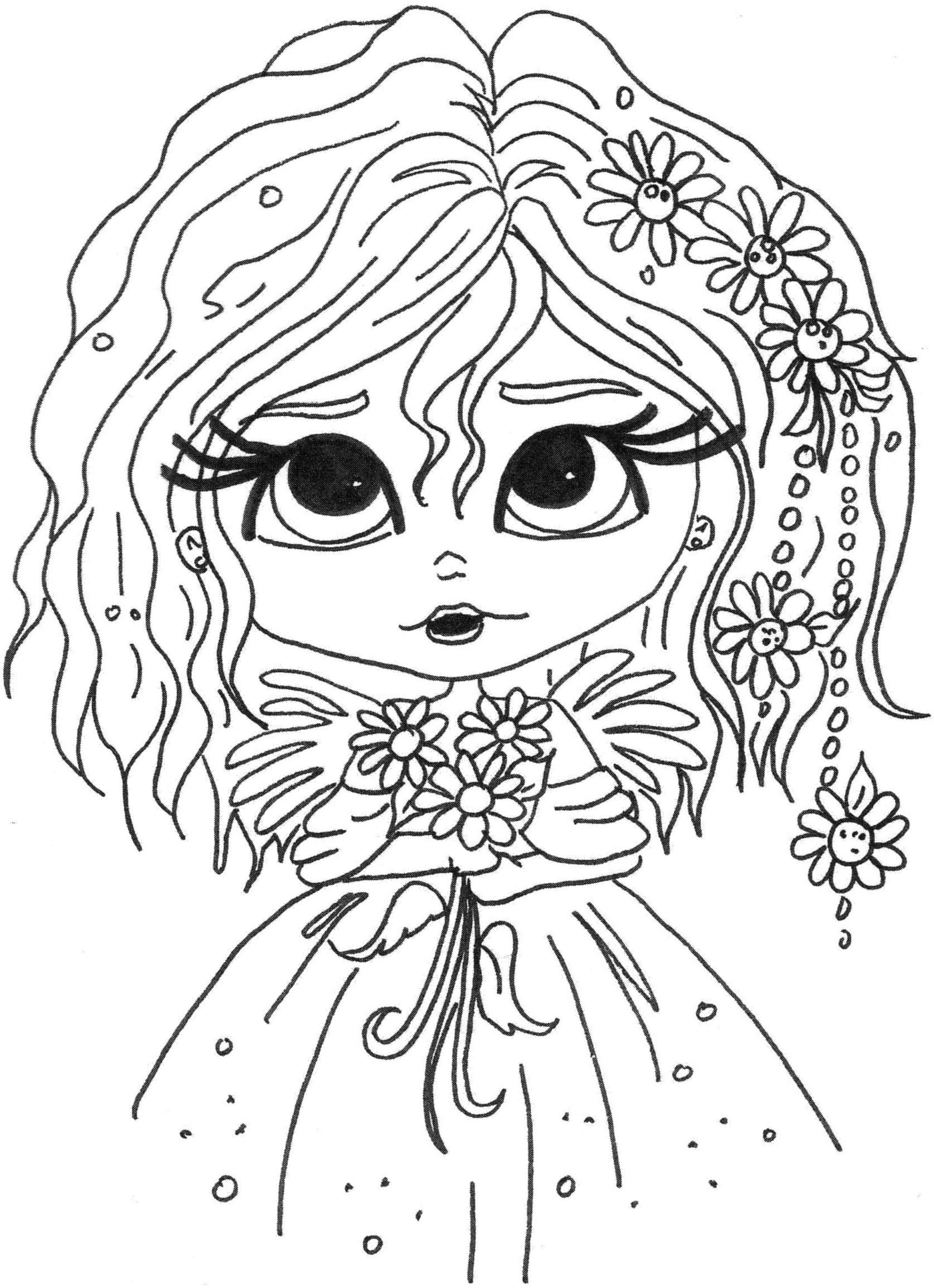

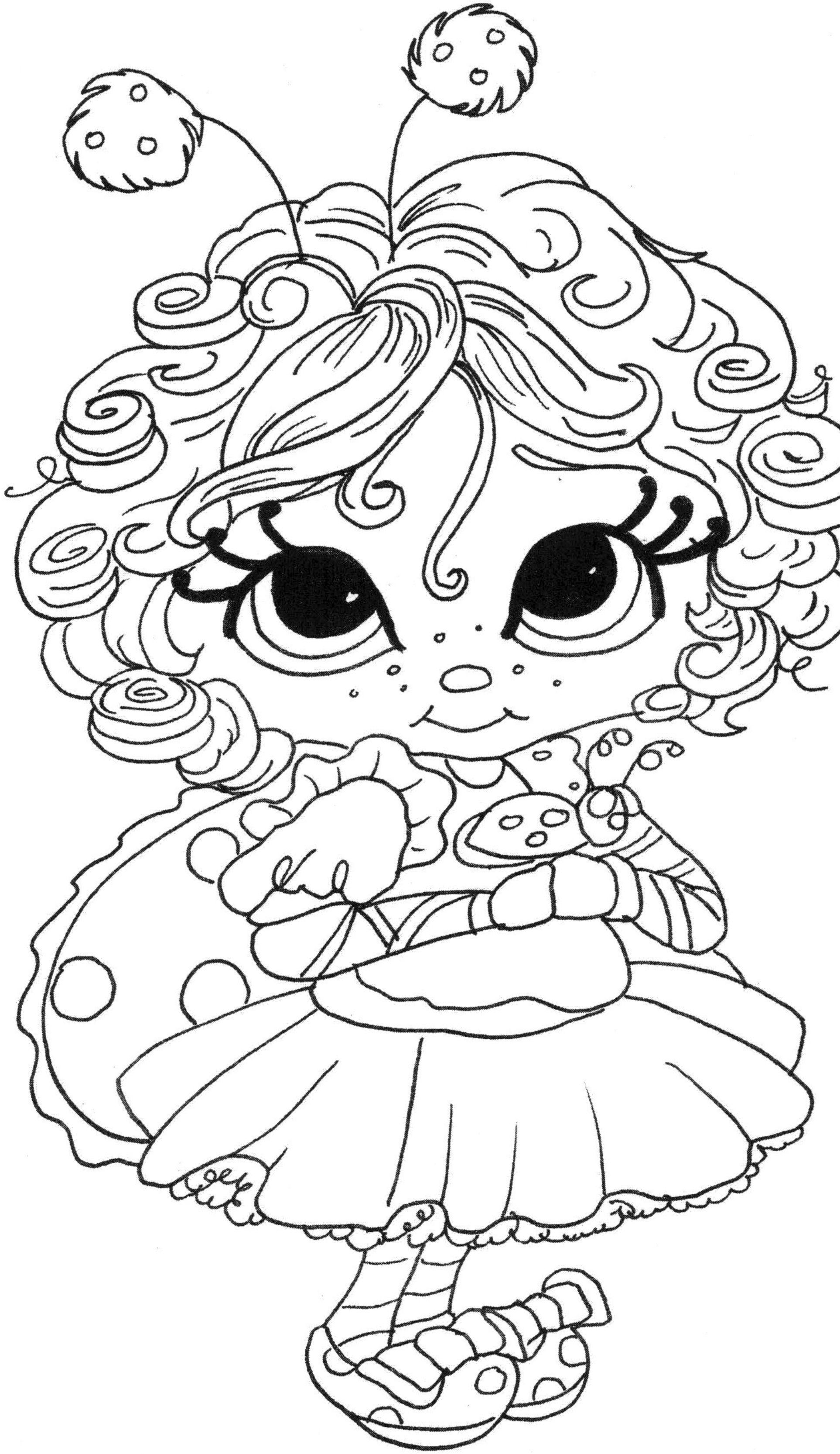

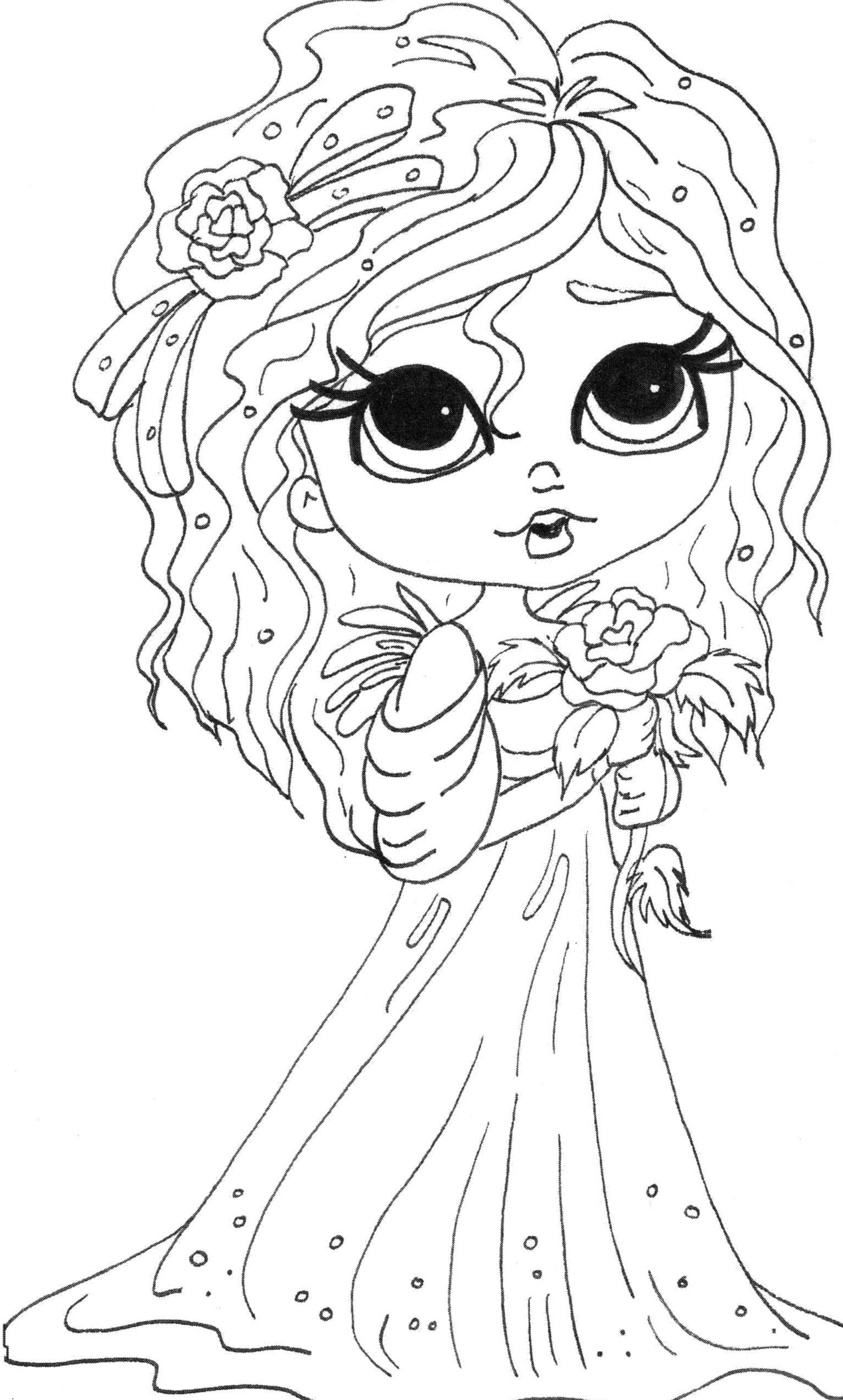

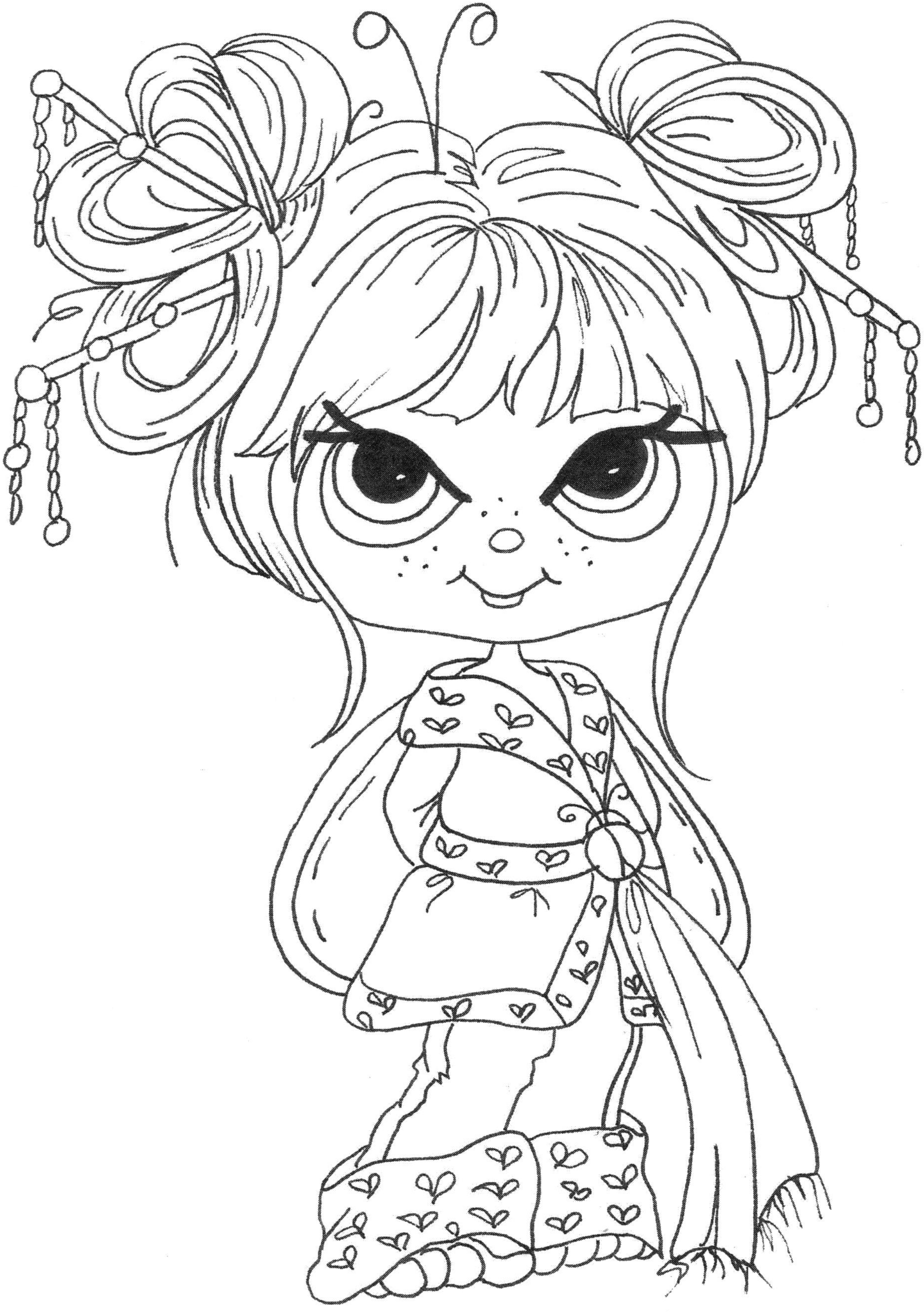

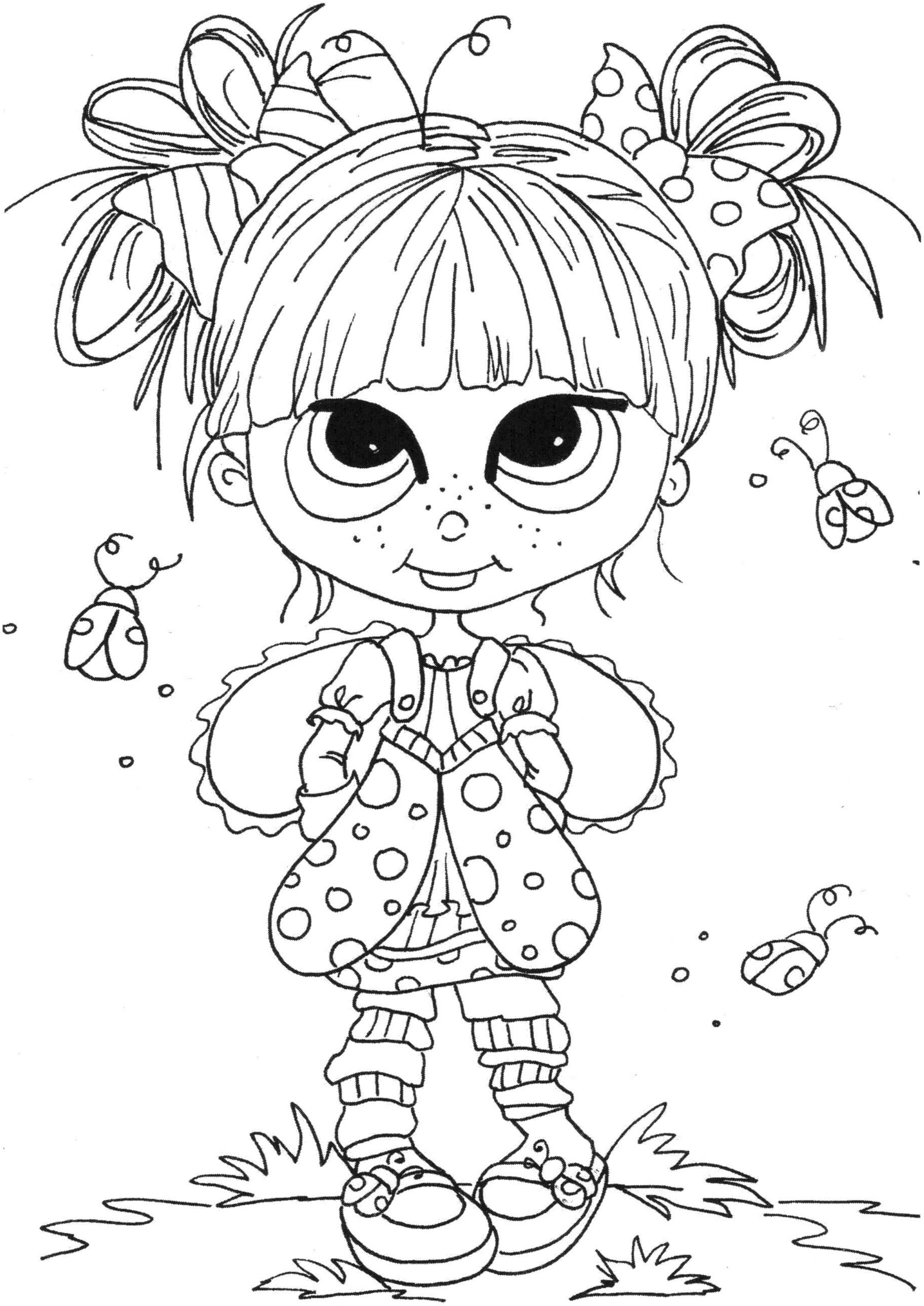

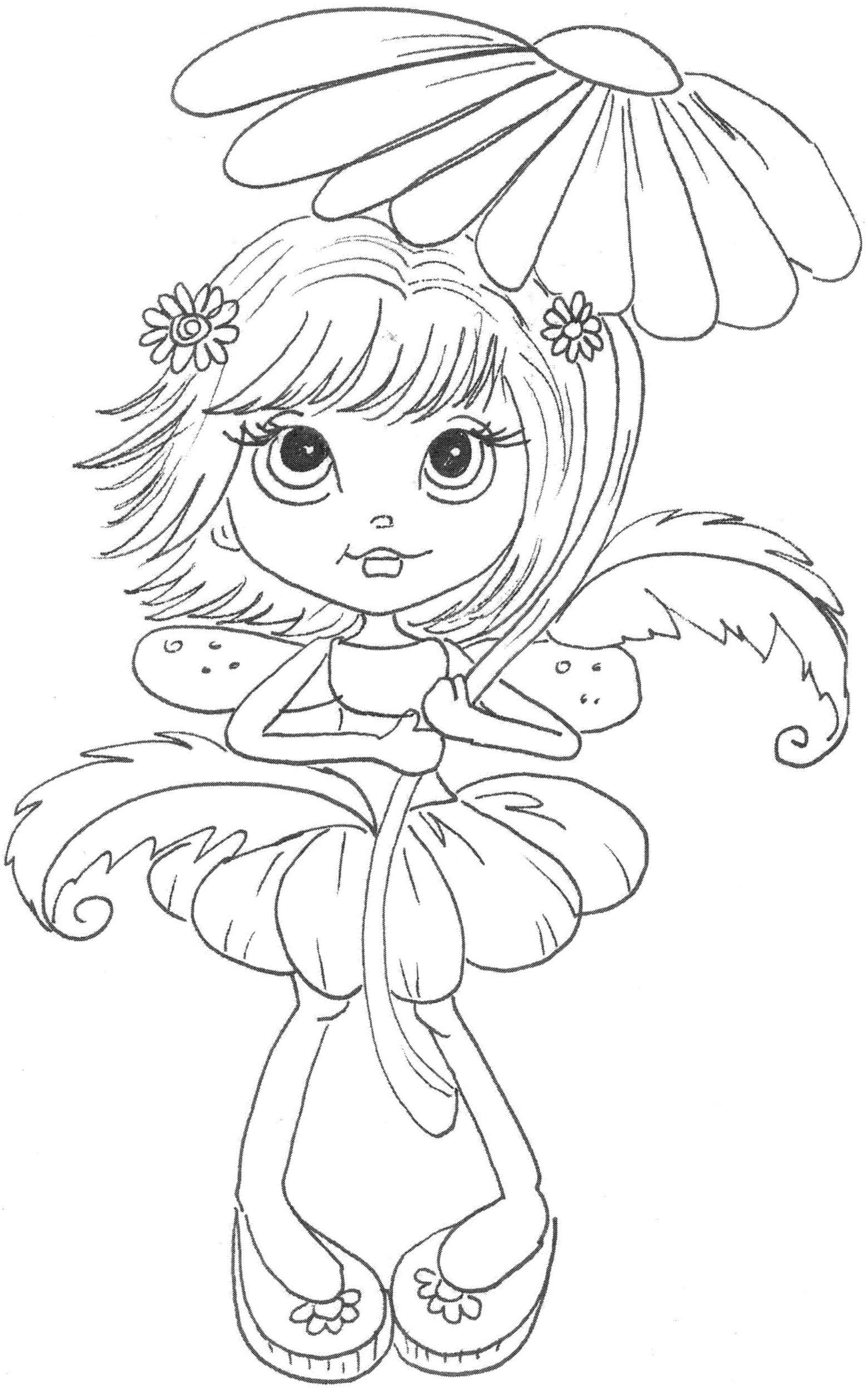

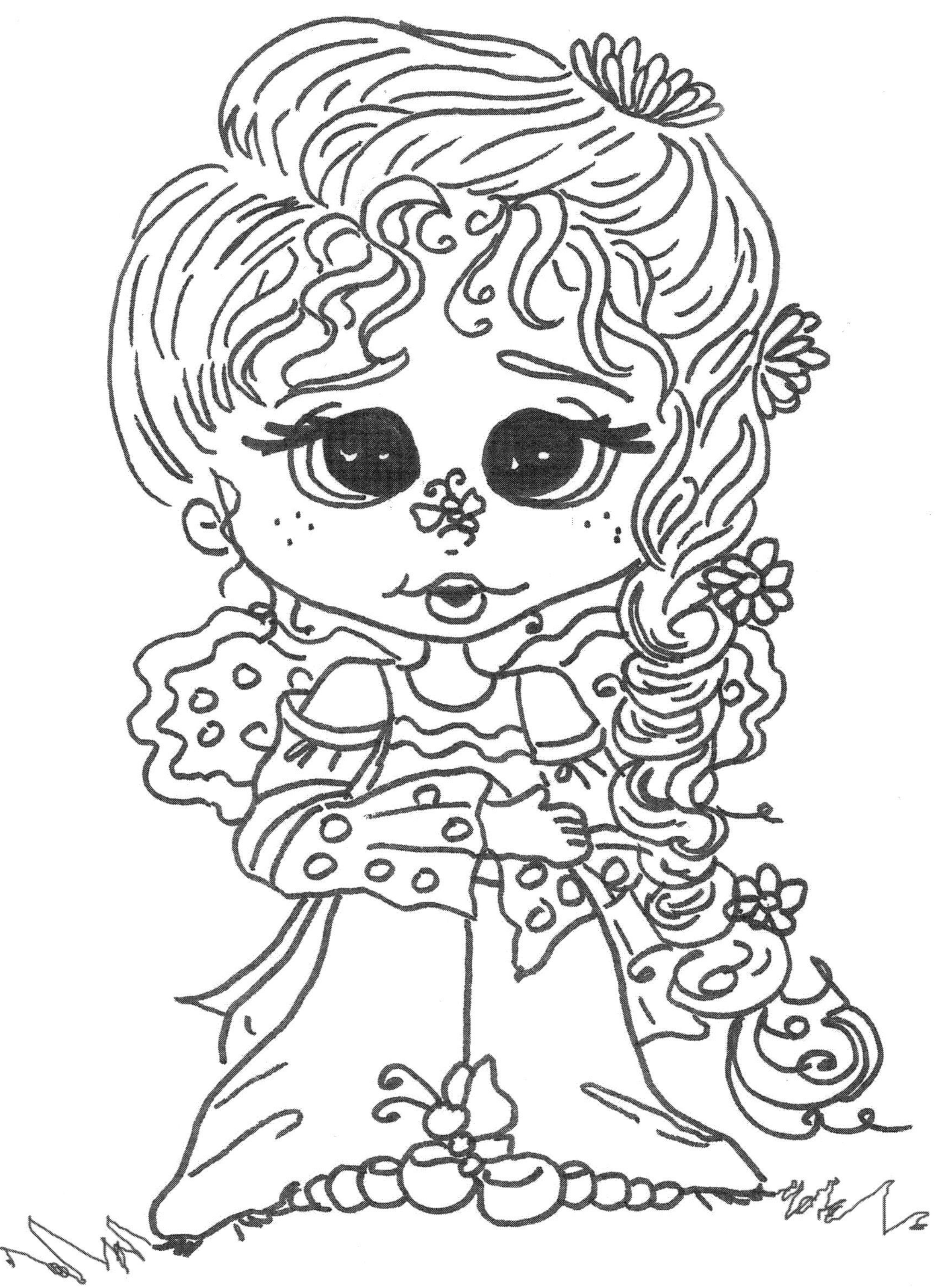

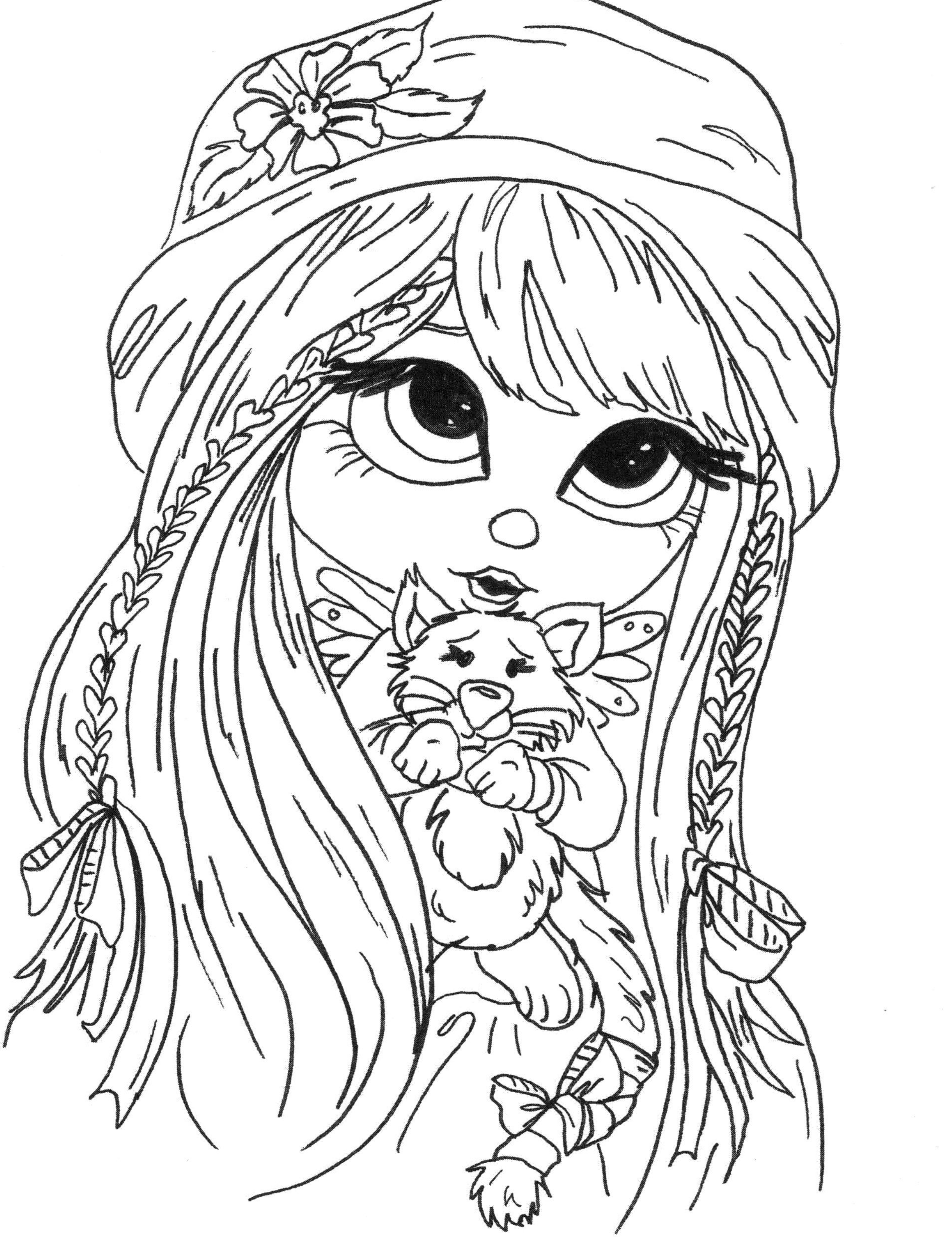

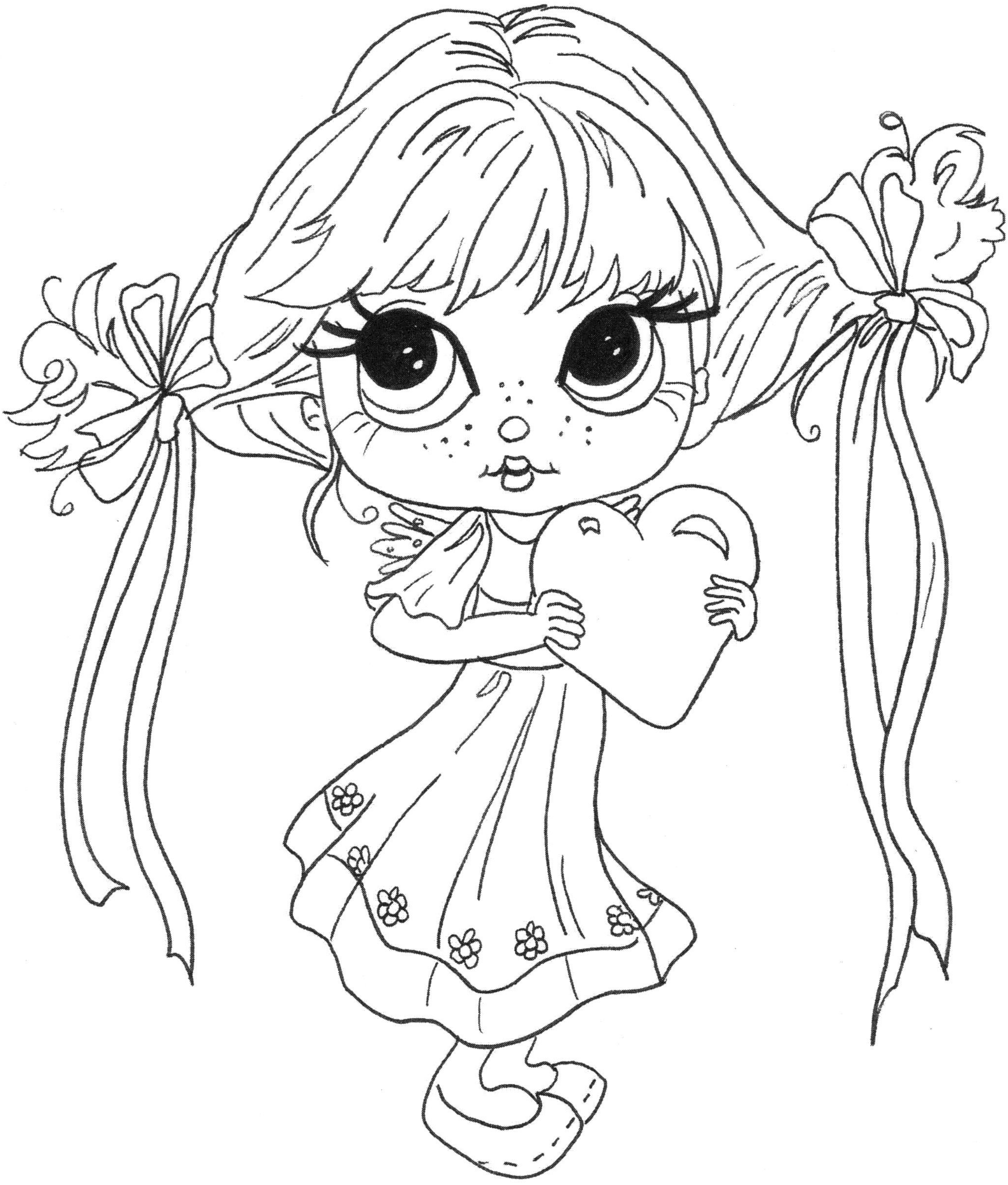

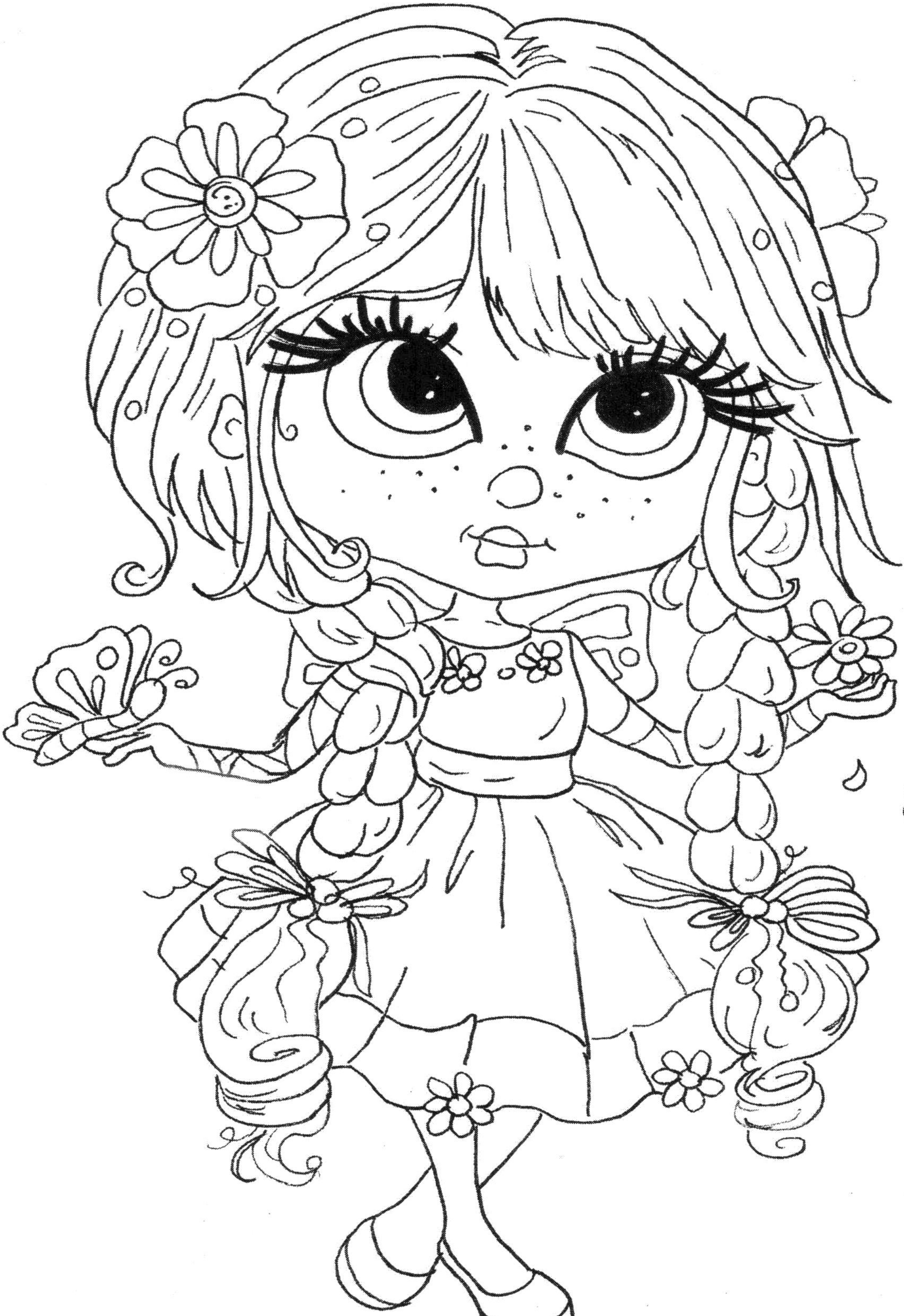

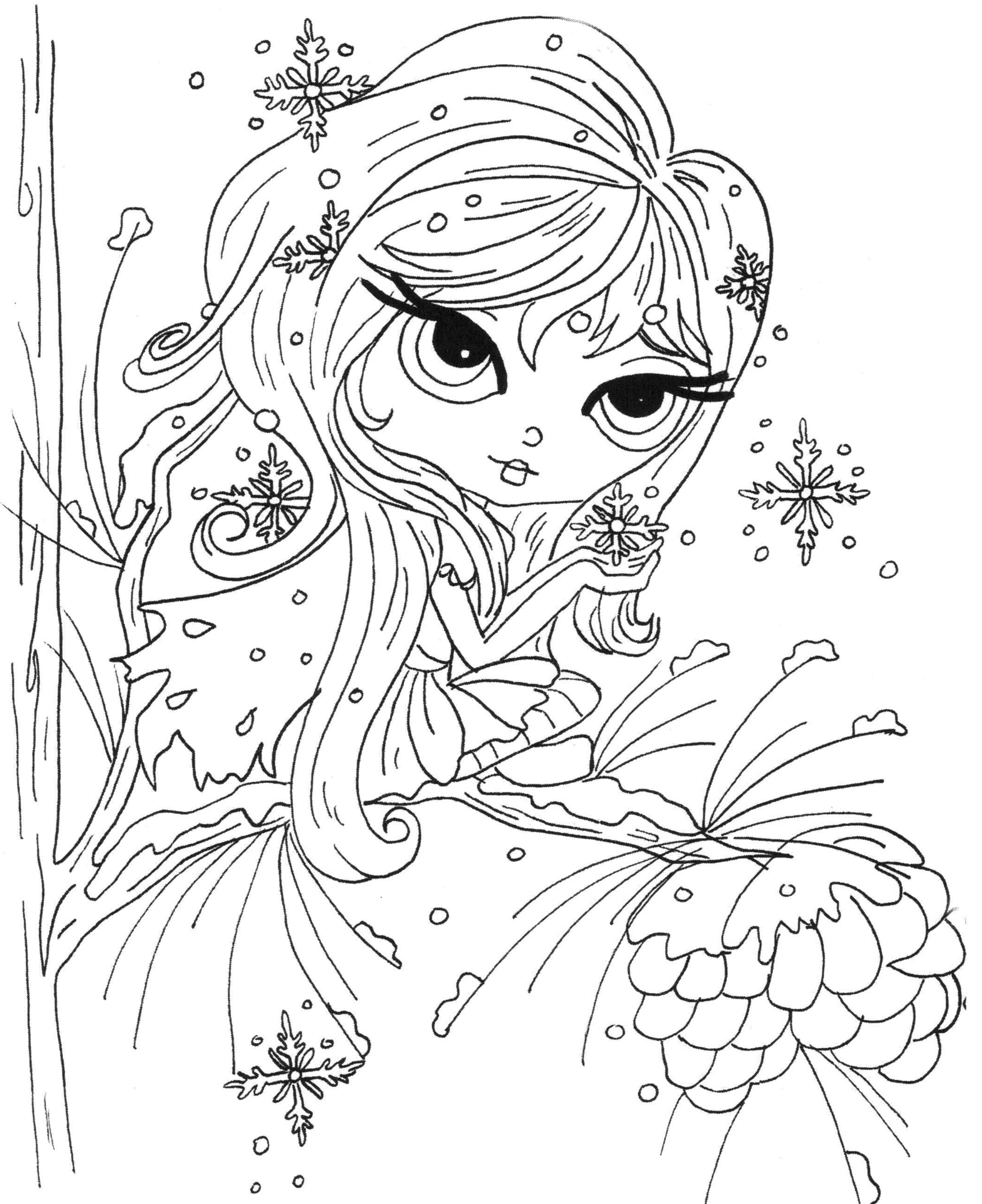

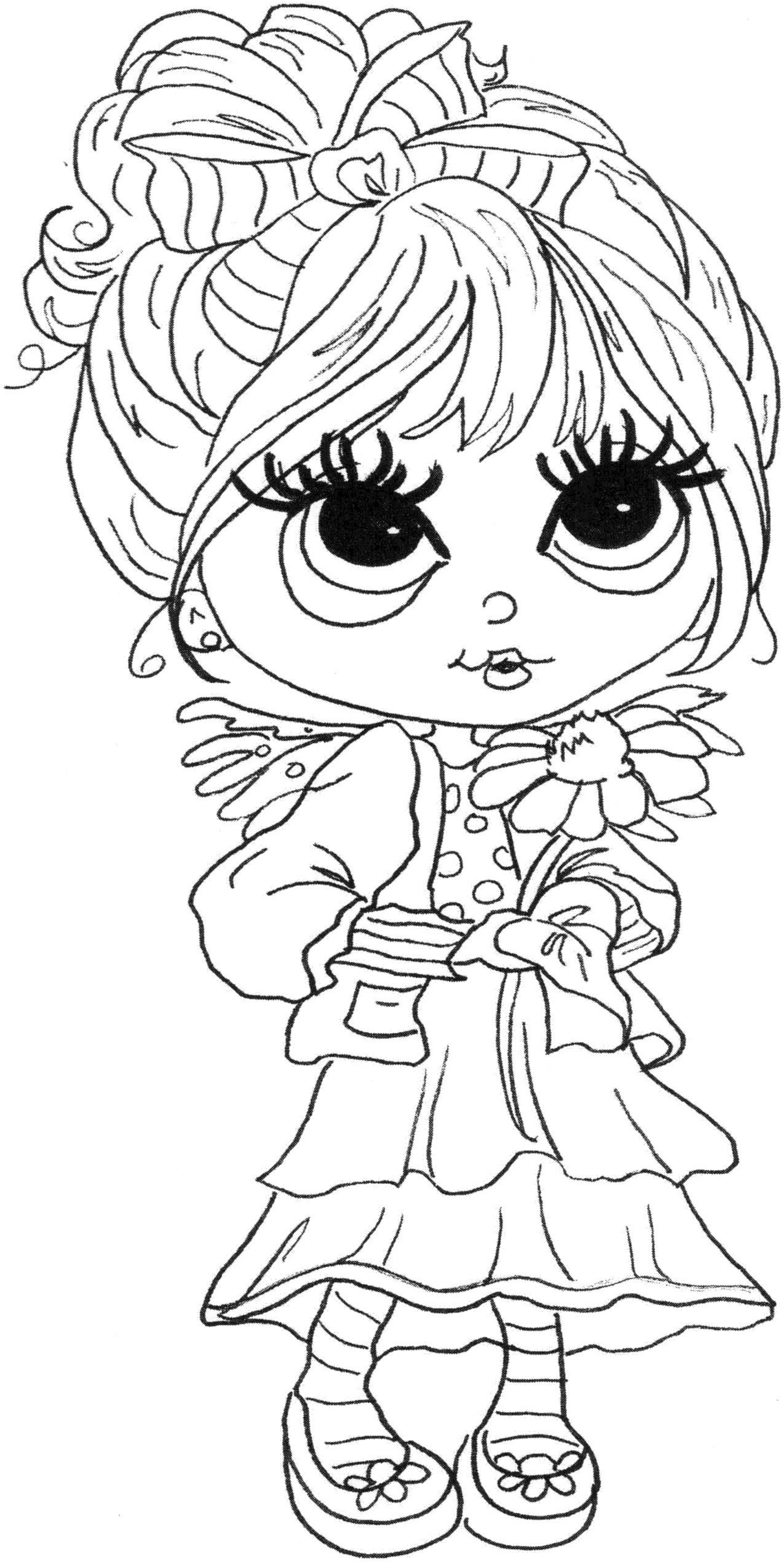

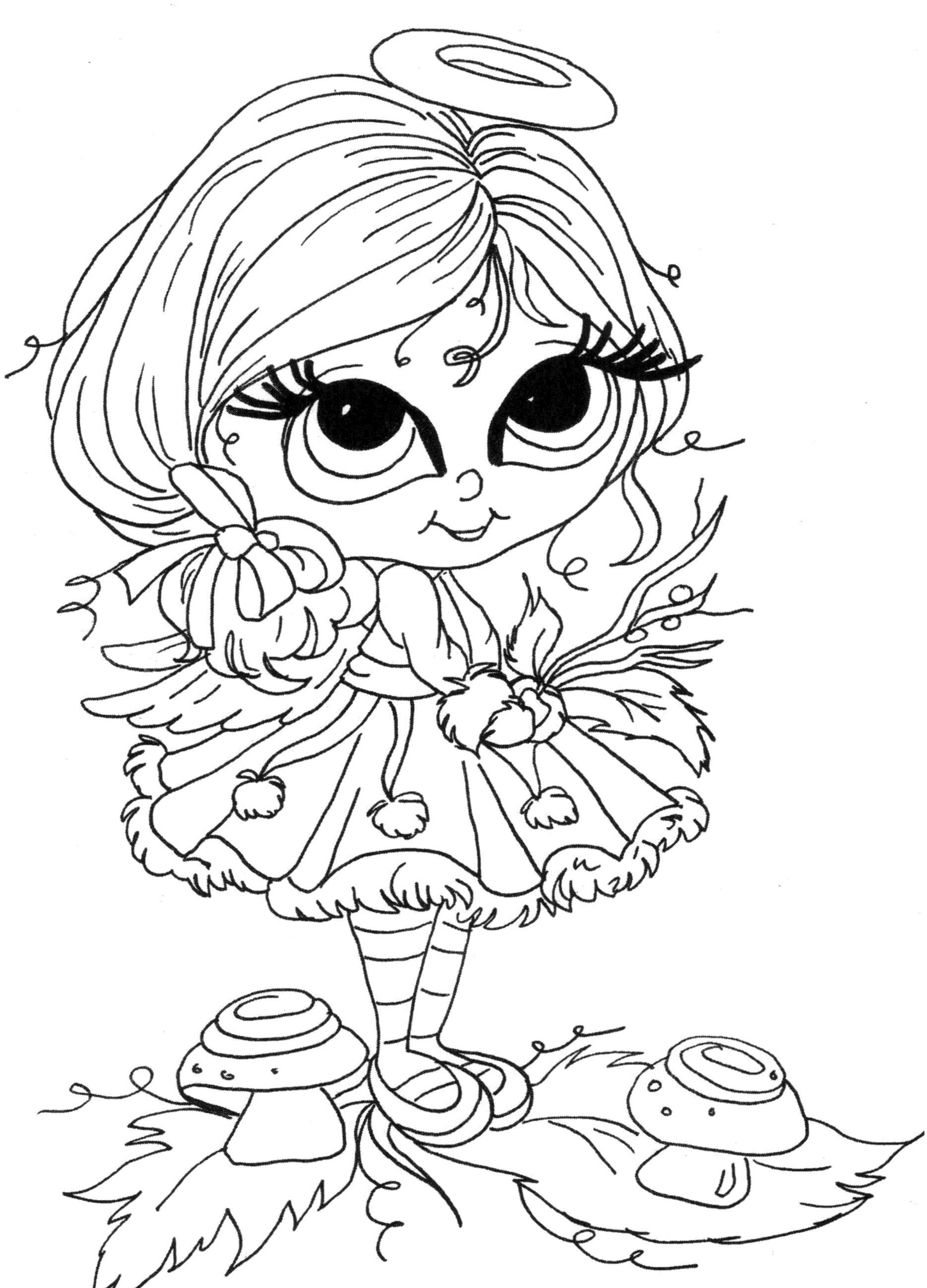

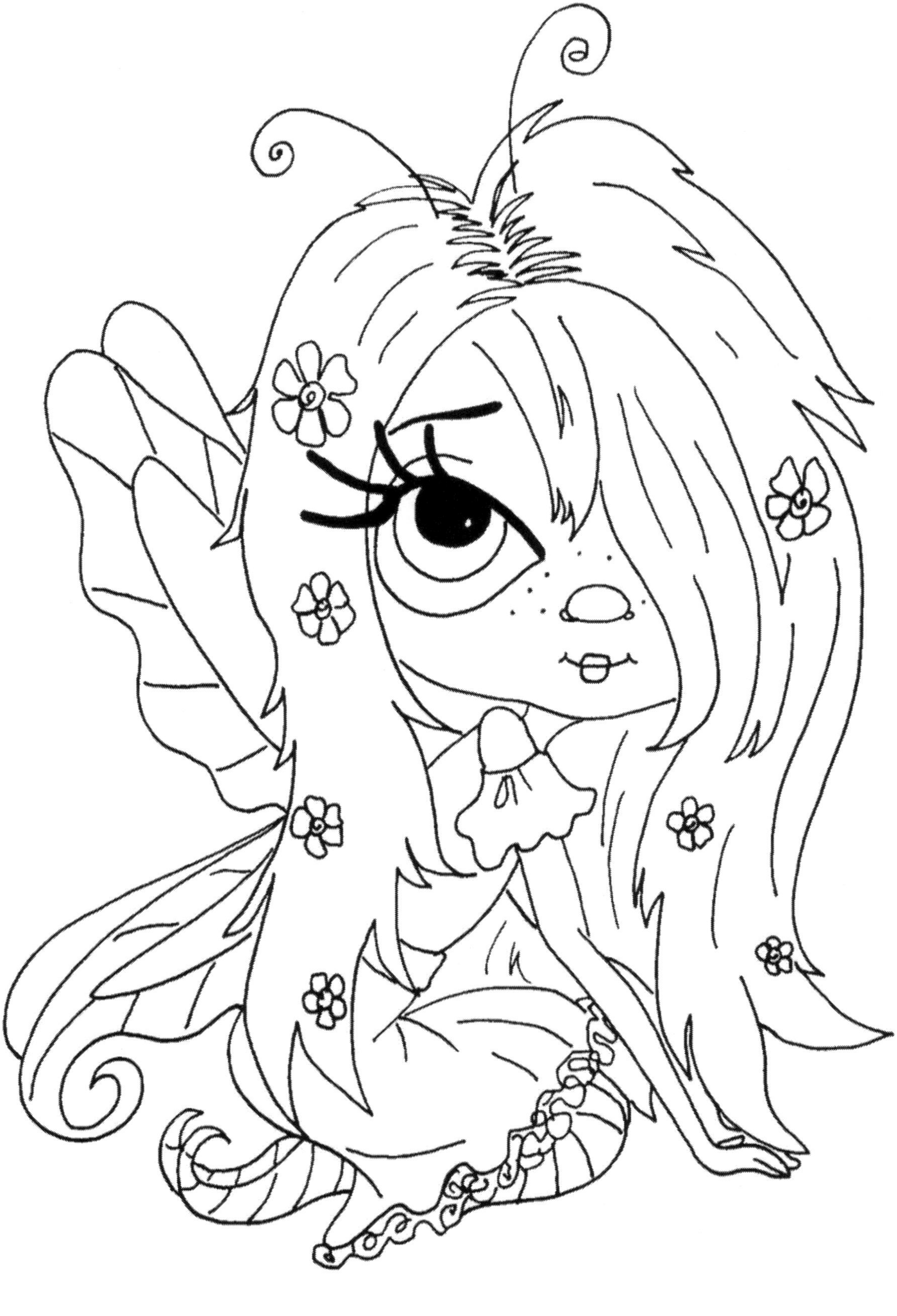

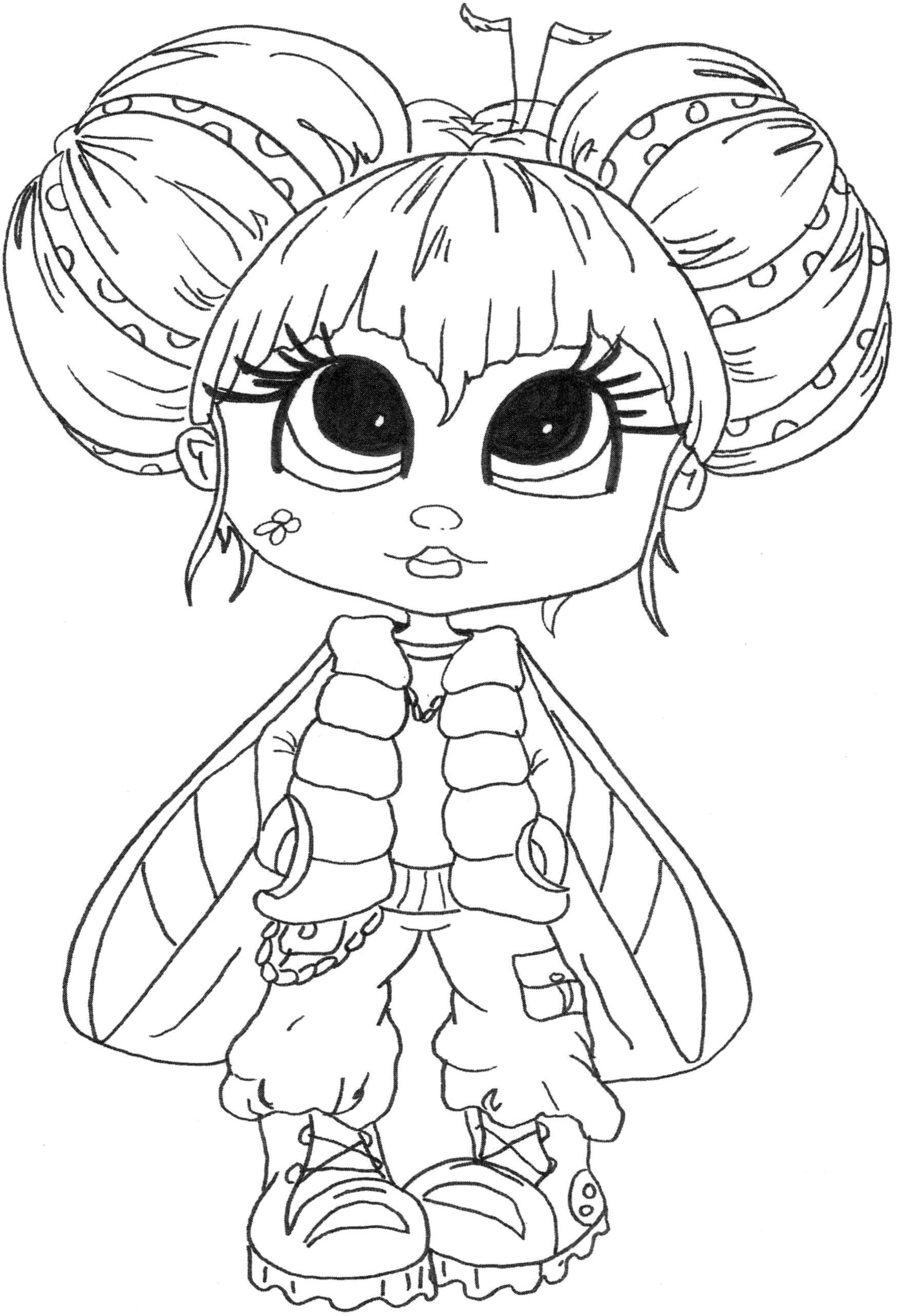

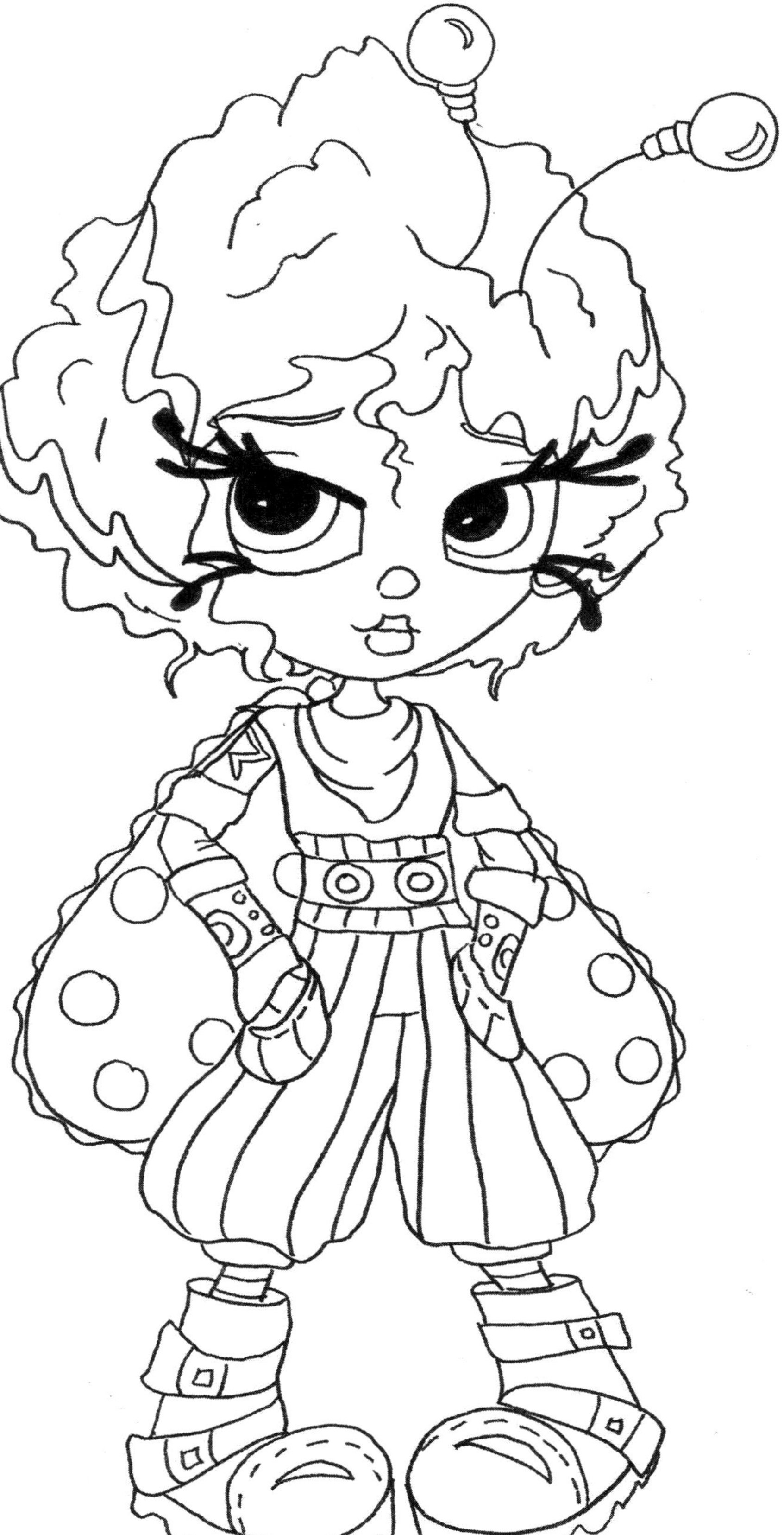

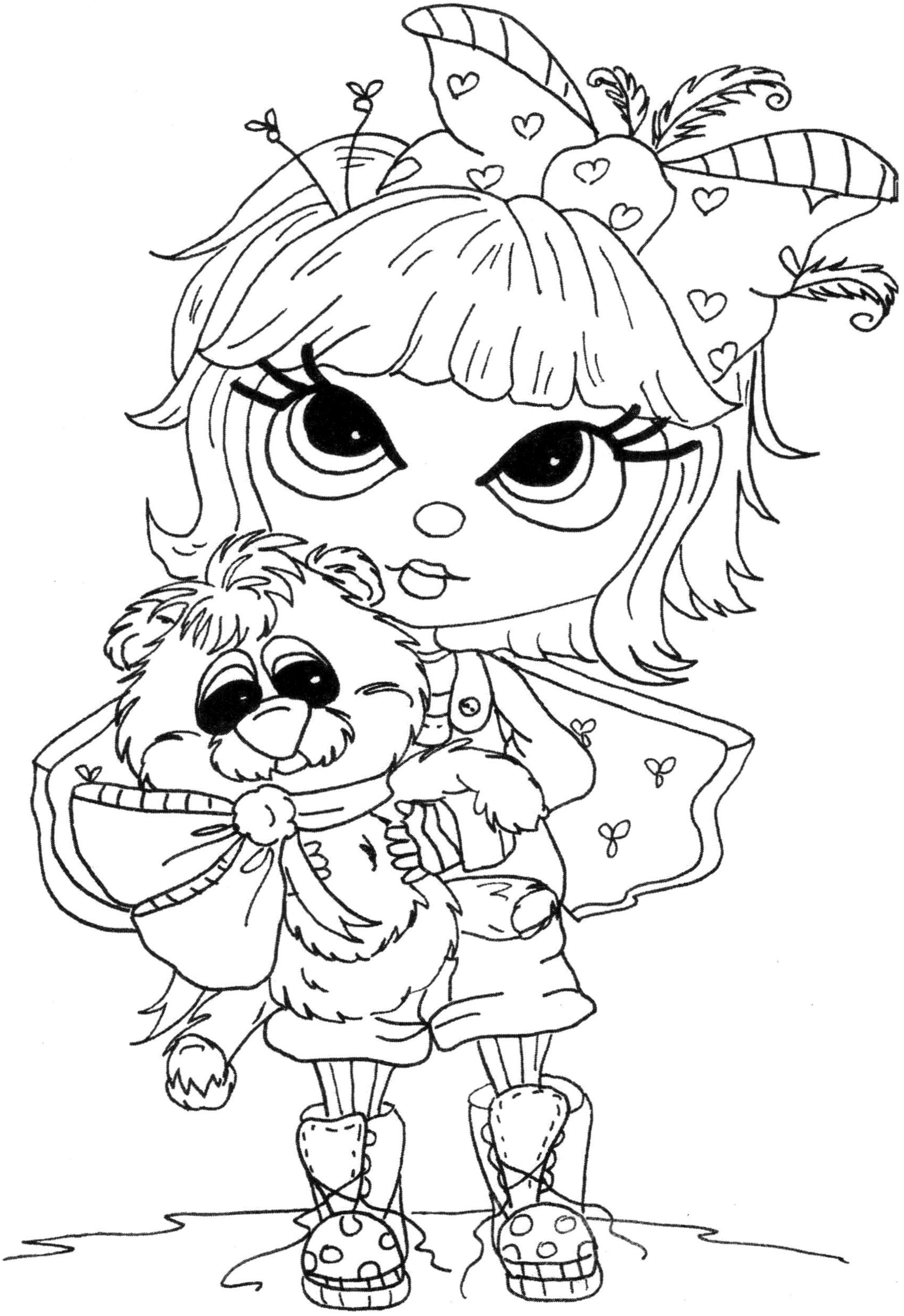

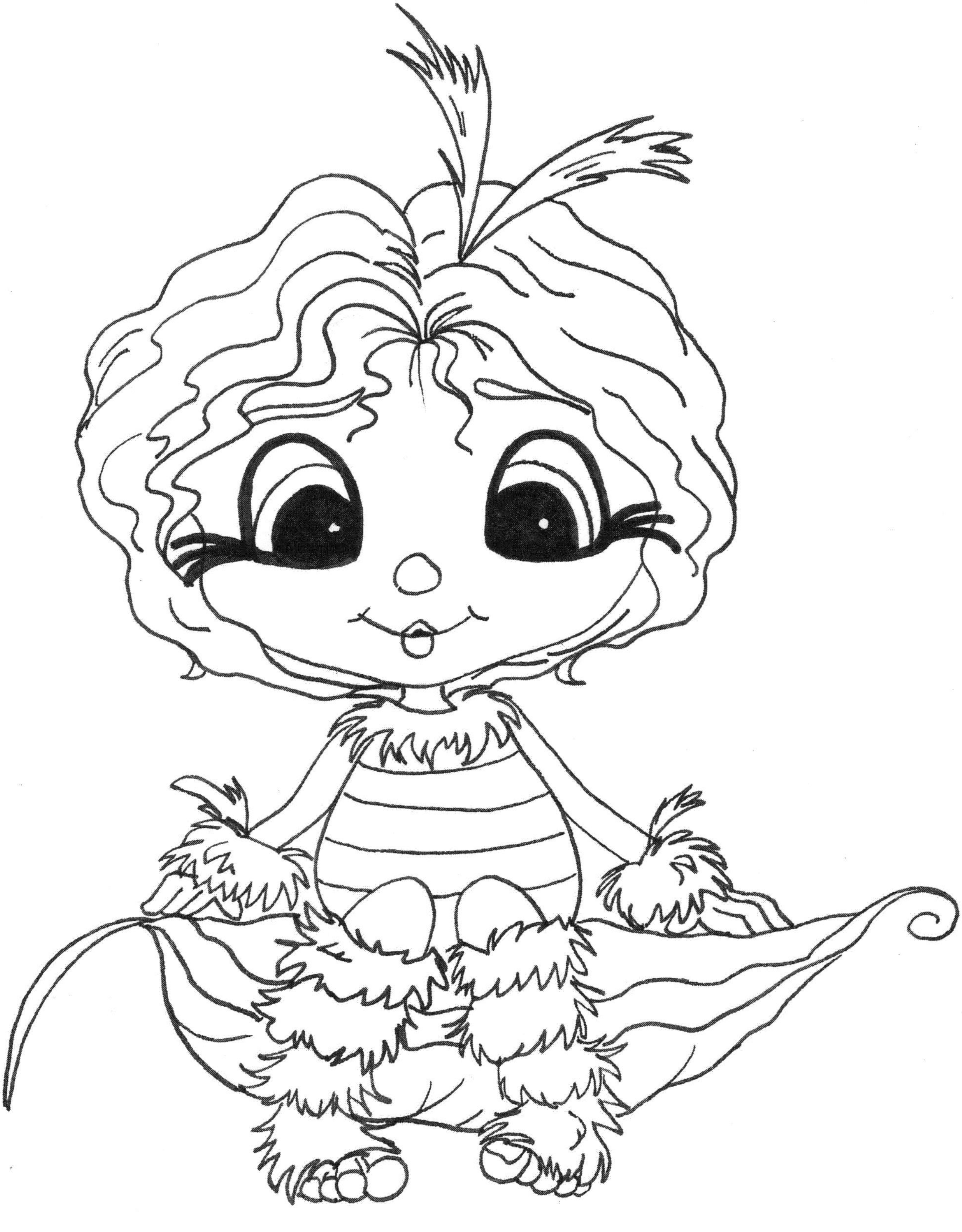

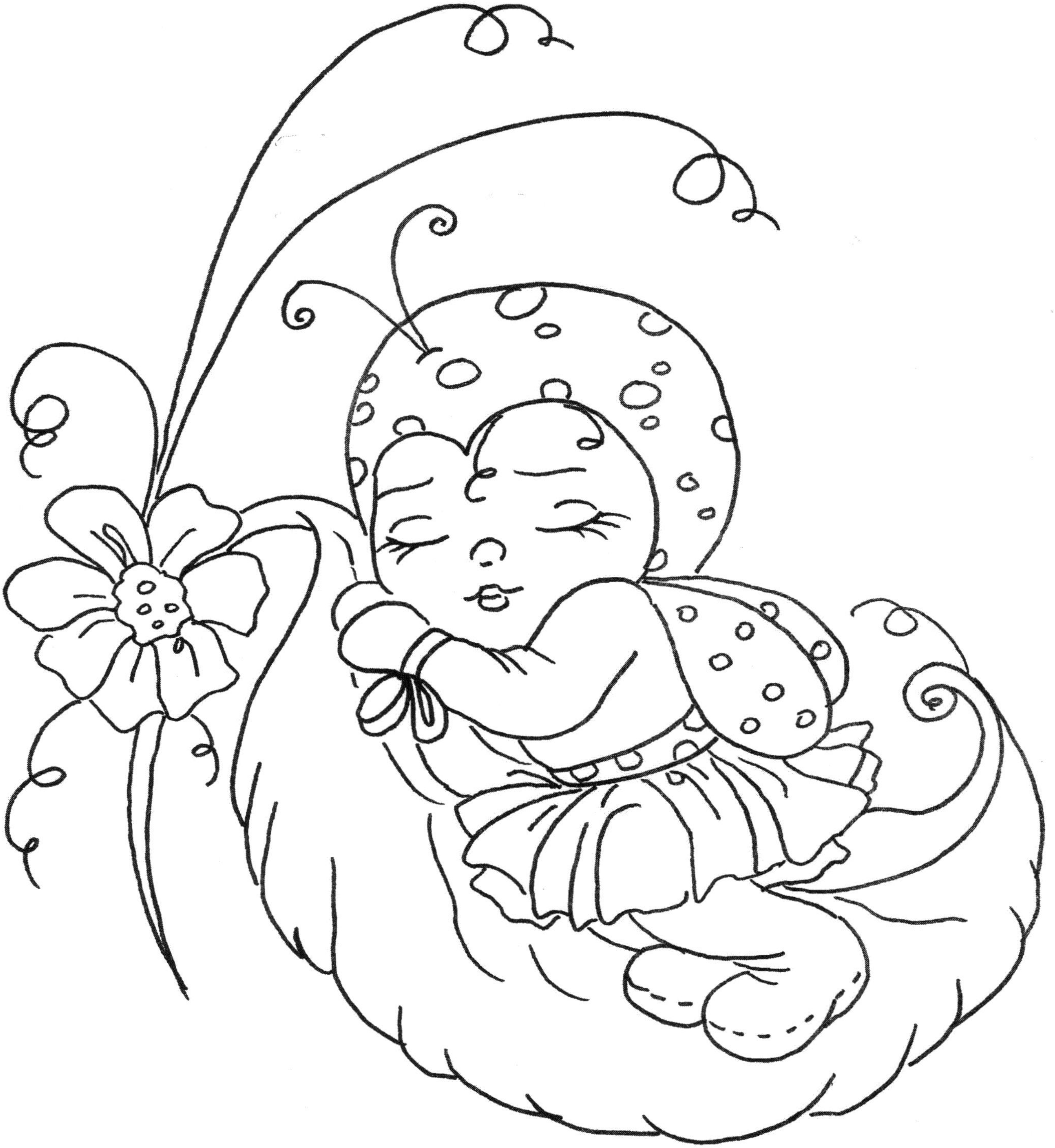

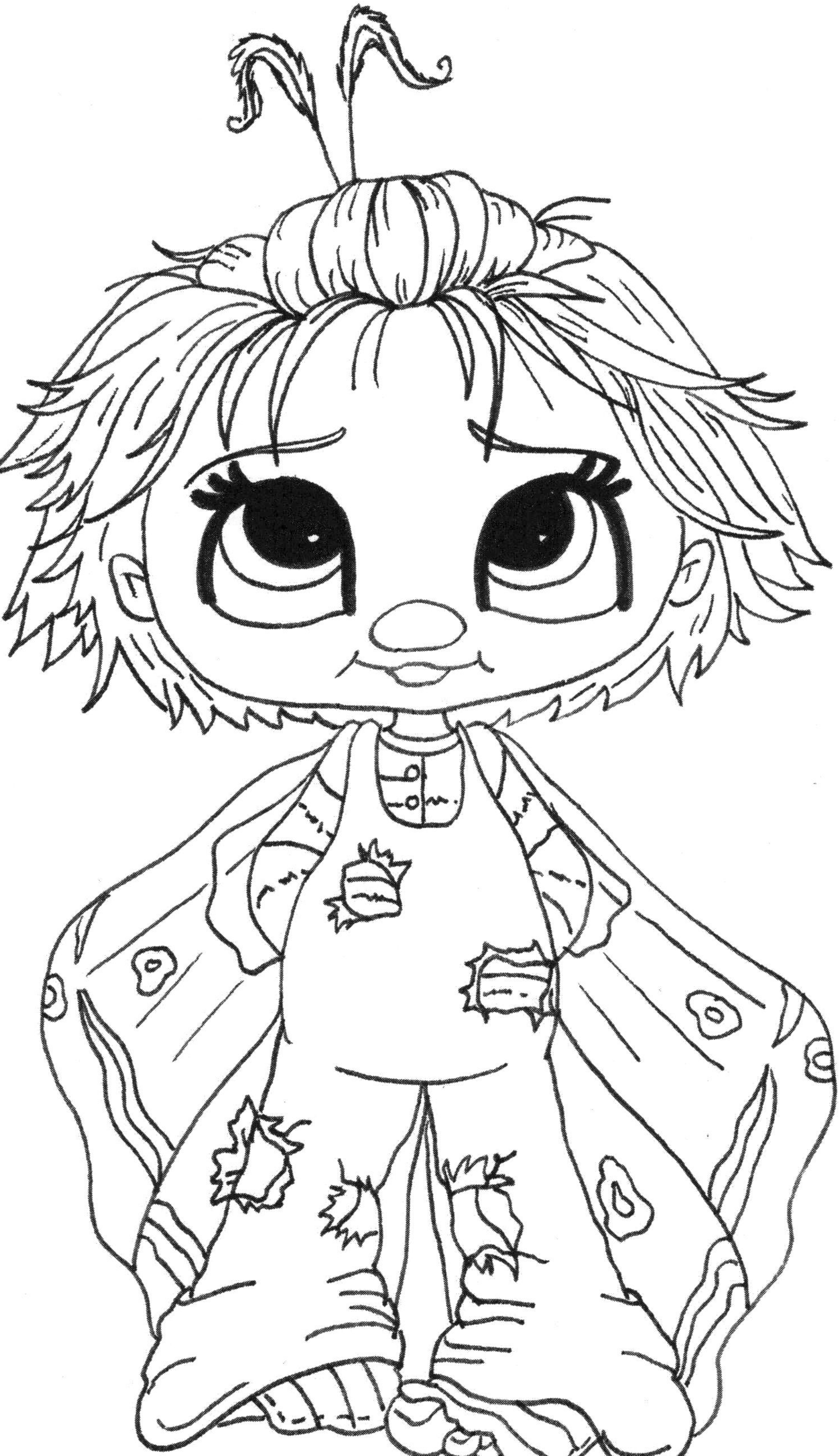

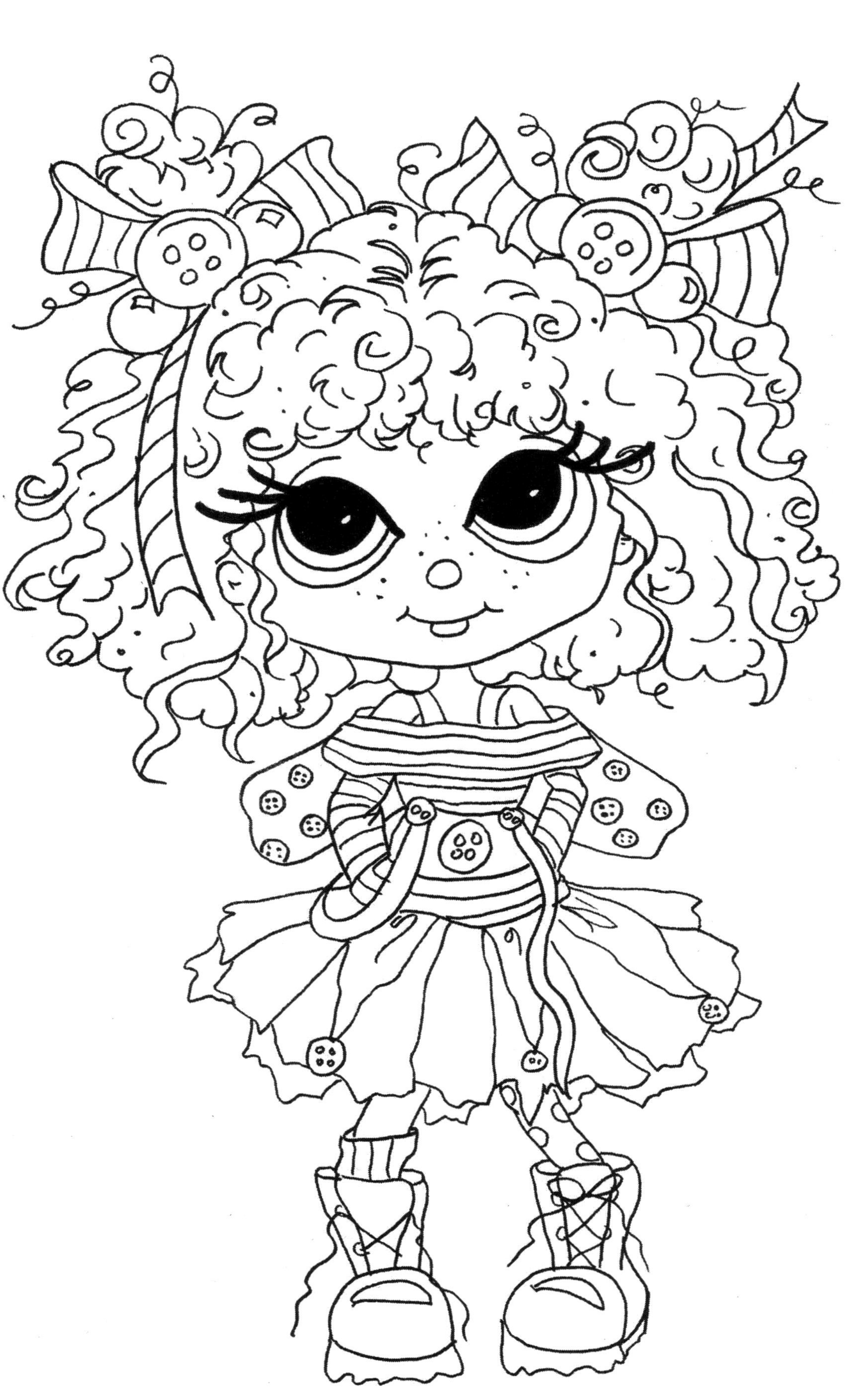

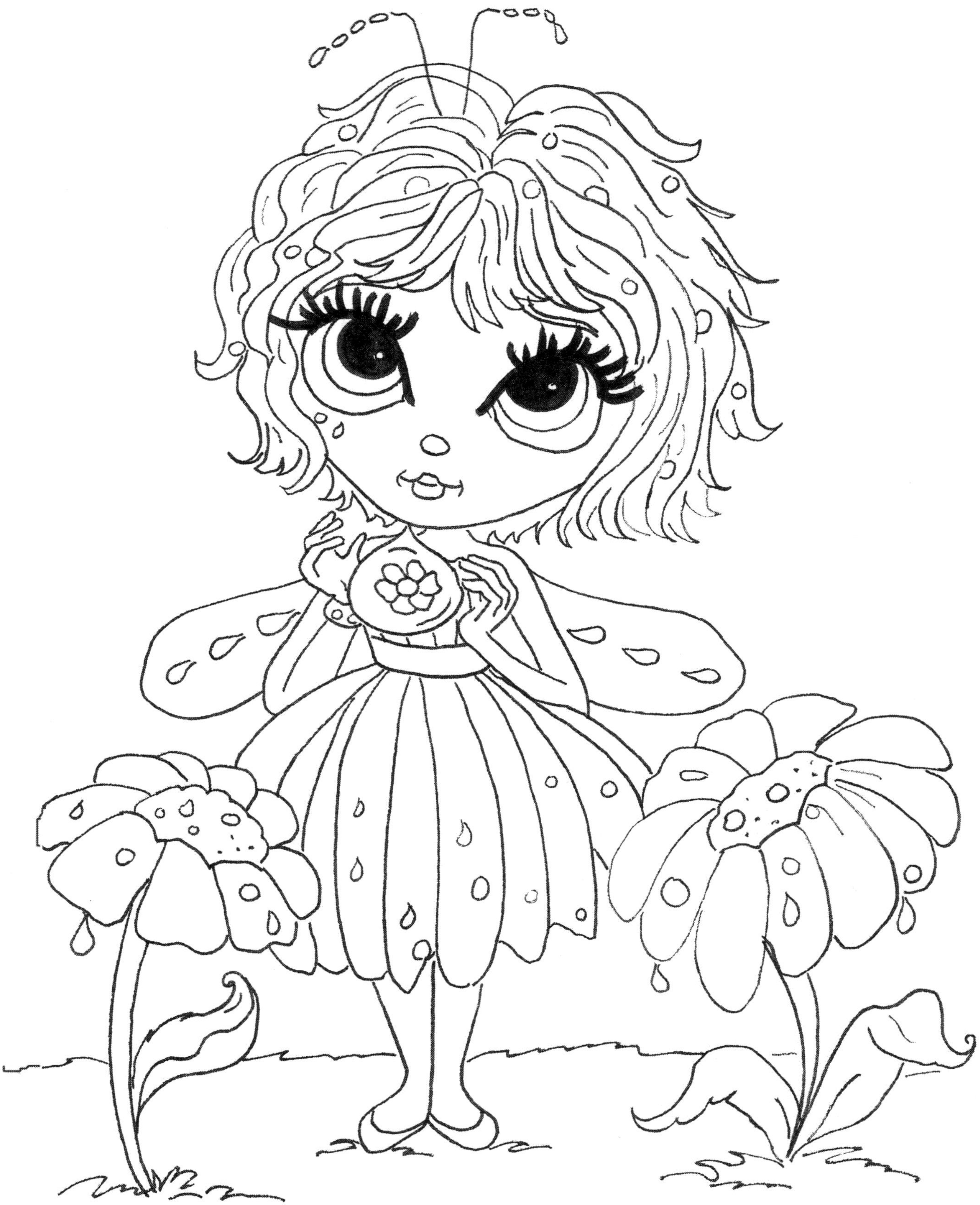

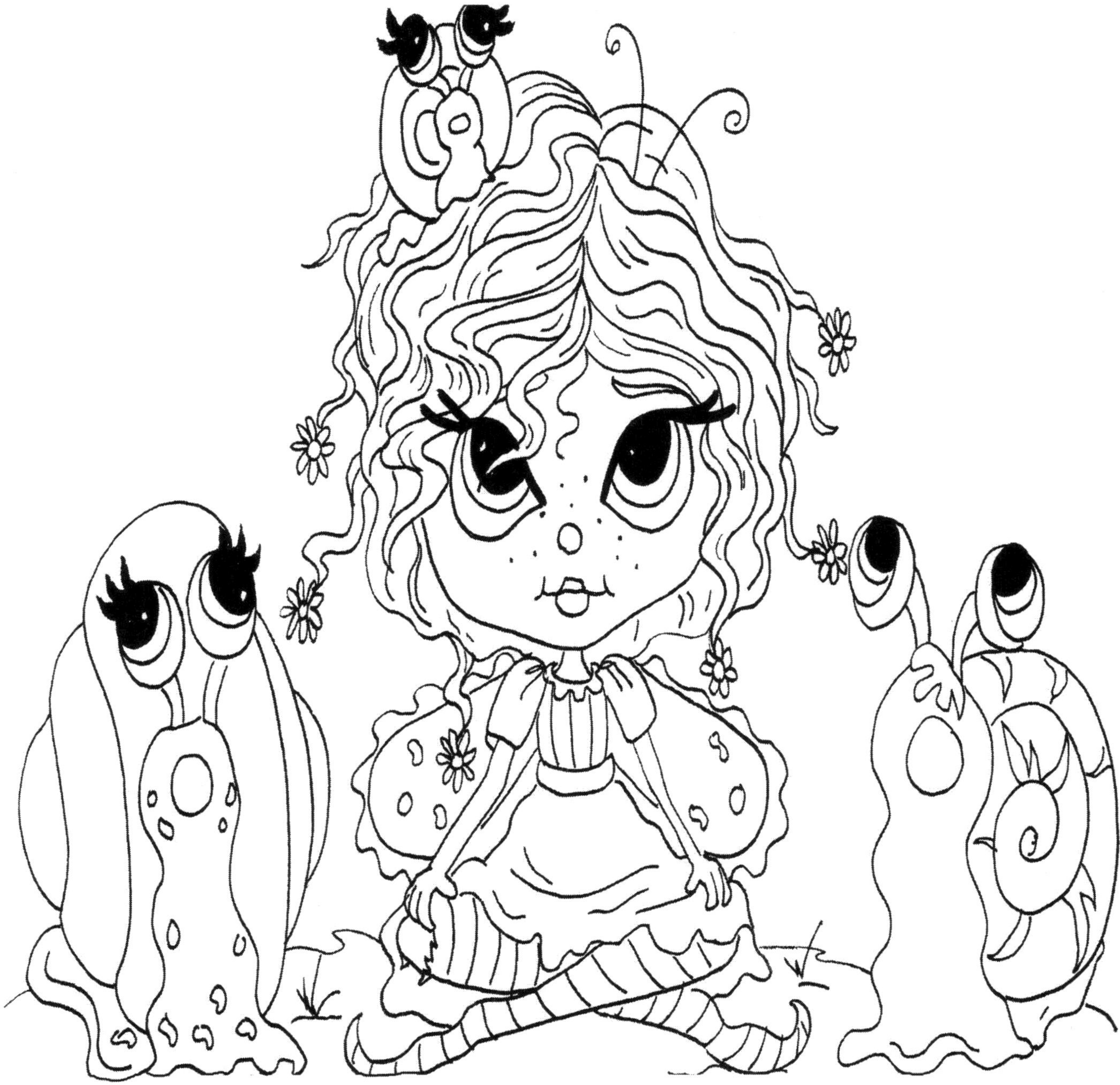

65600658R00046

Made in the USA
Middletown, DE
01 March 2018